FOREST AND CPR MANAGEMENT IN EASTERN HIMALAYAS

FOREST AND CPR MANAGEMENT IN EASTERN HIMALAYAS

A. IBOTOMBI SINGH

AKANSHA PUBLISHING HOUSE
NEW DELHI-110002 (INDIA)

AKANSHA PUBLISHING HOUSE
4649-B/21, Ansari Road
Darya Ganj, New Delhi - 110 002
Email: ektabooks@yahoo.com
Ph. : 23263193/9811582579/94351167 18
Visit us: www.akanshpublishinghouse.com

Forest & CPR Management in Eastern Himalayas

First Published 2010

Reprint-2026

ISBN 978-81-8370-198-3

PRINTED IN INDIA

Published by M.P. Misra for Akansha Publishing House, New Delhi

Dedicated to the
unprivileged villagers of
Anjaw
and
Lohit Districts
of
Arunachal Pradesh

Contents

Foreword

I am happy to present and introduce this book on "Forest and CPR Management in Eastern Himalayas" by Dr. A. Ibotombi Singh. This book is an outcome of his Doctoral research project on a very relevant topic in the context of Arunachal Pradesh.

An increasing interest in environmental economics has led to a great deal of research works in recent years on the economics of local common property resources (CPRs). Since the historical past, CPRs play a crucial role in the economy of Arunachal Pradesh. With a population of only 10.91 lakhs (as per 2001 census) Arunachal Pradesh is a home of twenty-six major tribes and 110 sub-tribes. Agriculture – the main occupation of people of the State is of two types: (i) shifting cultivation based on slash and burn method which is locally known as *jhumming* where land is communally held and the individual member derives usufructuary rights of the land he cultivates and (ii) permanent cultivation where individual property rights have been well established. For the indigenous population of Arunachal Pradesh shifting cultivation is supplemented by hunting and food gathering in the common forests, pastures, ponds, rivers etc. Their life is intimately linked with forest which is their well loved home and sources of livelihood.

In the post-Independence period, the launch of development activities by the Government has brought about significant changes in the communal economy of the State. Under mutually reinforcing influence of Government sponsored urbanization, development of human capital and market penetration, the economy of

Arunachal Pradesh has witnessed many structural and institutional changes including the individualization of communally held land and forests.

With this background, Dr. Singh attempts to study the impact of household-level heterogeneity on the degree and nature of forest depending under conditions of declining forest cover and institutional diversity. In fact, the basic objective of the study was to understand the relationship between household's socio-economic characteristics and consumption from forests in order to investigate whether the gradual shift to property rights has enhanced or restricted the access of poorer households to the local commons. Based on household level data from nine villages in the two districts of Arunachal Pradesh, the study brings out the significance of forest resources as a source of livelihood in Arunachal Pradesh.

I am sure that this book will contribute to the growing body of literature in the area of economics of common property resources of the country as a whole and in Arunachal Pradesh and other North-East Indian States in particular. The book will be a valuable source of information for the environmental economists, environmentalists and finally the policy makers.

PROF. AMITAVA MITRA
Head, Department of Economics
Rajiv Gandhi University, Itanagar
Arunachal Pradesh.

Preface

The indigenous tribal communities living on forest fringes or within forests in the picturesque Eastern Himalayas are not only maintaining the forest eco-system for generations but also the survival of these communities depend their daily needs on the community forests. A common perception that the high dependency of these communities are the major cause of degradation and depletion of natural resources base seems to be far from reality since this area exhibits a high percentage of forest cover. However, institutional arrangements evolve along with changes in the structure of political economy. During transitions from common or community property rights regime to private property regime the institutional structures of community-based institution for natural resource management are expected to change as well. The implications of these changes will not be uniform across the different rural classes, primarily because as theoretical and empirical evidences suggest, privatization of commons is often accompanied by increasing inequality in the distribution of resources. The key questions that have been investigated, in such a context are: Are there any differences in consumption value from community forest between poor and non-poor households? Does the institution-based CPR management results in extraction of more or less forest products? Does this form of forest management improve the welfare of poor households? How do the individual members of the rural community and households change their livelihood strategies in response to these institutional changes?

Arunachal Pradesh, the Eastern Himalayan State, has witnessed large-scale changes in the property rights structure as well as natural resource base. Therefore, community forests offers a unique opportunity to study these enquiries in greater detail. The results are not only expected to clarify the theoretical issues of relationship between Common Property Resource (CPR) management and its distributional aspects in rural settings but also may contribute towards developing a more sophisticated policy response towards better participatory resource management. In fact, there have been a number of theoretical and empirical studies on the successes and failures of CPR management. However, there are a few studies that have paid attention to equity, equality and its distributional implications of common property institutions as well as rural livelihood strategies in general and the eastern Himalayan State in particular.

I duly acknowledge the help received from the staff of the various libraries, which I had visited during the course of the study. I am thankful to the staff of different libraries particularly, Rajiv Gandhi University, Itanagar, North East Hill University, Shillong, North Eastern Council, Shillong, Indian Council of Social Science and Research, Shillong, Manipur University, Imphal, OKD Institute for Social Change and Research, Guwahati, Gauhati University, Guwahati, Indian Council for Social Science Reasearce, Shillong, Dera Natung Government College, Itanagar, District Statistical Office (Statistics), Tezu and Directorate of Economics and Statistics Department, Government of Arunachal Pradesh, Itanagar. I owe my sincere gratitude to Mr. K. Manai, Research Officer, Economics and Statistics Department, Government of Arunachal Pradesh, Itanagar and Mr. K. Zaman Barbhuiya, Field Investigator, District Statistical Office, Lohit District, Tezu for their untiring help in providing all related statistical documents.

Perhaps my greatest debt is to the surveyed villages of Anjaw and Lohit districts of Arunachal Pradesh. I can imagine few things more humbling than the warmth and hospitality of people in such circumstances. Countless people in the surveyed villages opened their lives, shared their homes and spent hours together in helping me to understand the intricacies of their communities and livelihoods.

I wish to thank to Mr. Lollen Bellai, Mr. Sonue Bellai and Mr. Sotetlum Bellai with whom I went through steep mountains and dense forests following foot tracks to reach all the three scattered and remote villages of Brailiang, Kaniliang and Kasanglat in Anjaw district. Without their generous help, I would have been unable to accomplish even a fraction of work what I did. I owe them and their kith and kin a profound debt of gratitude for their generosity and hospitality. I was humbled by the warmth and generosity of *Gaon Burahs* and not only did they spend endless hours, despite their busy household chords and other activities, sharing their experience and insight with me, but they provided me a home and sense of belonging during my stay there. I also owe my gratitude to Mr. Soto Thalai of Wakro and Mr. Balijan Krisikro of Tillang Kyong village, Mr. Bagingso Pul of Karhe village and Mr. Sotheng Pul of Chireng village for helping me in translating local dialect to understand the household intricacies in Wakro Circle of Lohit district. I also owe my gratitude to all *Gaon Burahs* of Loiliang, Danglat and Tillang Kyong and *Village Chief* of Soolungtoo in Lohit district for their help in getting this work done. I also received invaluable help from my colleague Dr. M. Pathak, Lecturer in History, Indira Gandhi Government College, Tezu, Mr. Sabadam Tayang (APCS), Circle Officer, Dav Valley, Goiliang, Mr. Sanchit Ram Yadav, Junior Engineer, Public Works Department, Hayuliang, Mr. L. Maipak Singh, Deputy Superintendent of Police, Namsai Circle, Namsai who not only facilitated my stay but also helped in many ways to contact different local leaders of the area of study and arranging meetings and discussion. I am thankful to them for spending long hours with me and also allowing me to use their names in this book.

I owe my deep sense of gratitude and indebtedness to Professor Amitava Mitra, Head and Dean, Faculty of Social Sciences, Rajiv Gandhi University, Rono Hills, Itanagar for showing such interest in my work and progress, for coaching me through this amazing process of learning and self discovery, and for pushing me to do the best I ever could – from the very beginning to the very end.

It has been possible for me to complete this study because of the moral inspiration from my departed loving parents whose invisible guidance led me to this destination. I owe indebtedness to my learned colleagues, Dr. B.P. Sah, Dr. S.D. Jha and Dr. A.K. Pandey of Dera Natung Government College for their cooperation during this seemingly endless process. Special thanks also go to Madam D. Mitra for her cooperation, caring and endless encouragements during the work. I owe my gratitude to my brothers, sister, in-laws and nephews for making me feel that my work was important and for creating a loving environment in which I found the freedom to pursue this work. And my gratitude goes to my wife Dr. Suparna Bhattacharjee who has read every piece of this work. There are certainly no way I could have made it through this process without her companionship and love. I am also thankful to my daughter Baby A. Aena for her cooperation, patience and understandings.

Lastly, but not the least, I would like to thank Mr. M.P. Misra (CEO) of the Akansha Publishing House for taking keen interest in bringing out this book.

July 20, 2009 **Dr. A. IBOTOMBI SINGH**

List of Tables

List of Illustrations/Maps

ILLUSTRATIONS

MAPS

1

Introduction

Property rights structures influence the quality of forests through multiple channels of influences. It is being widely recognized now that participatory, decentralized and local level managements of natural resources through long-enduring community-based institutional arrangements may have some advantages over state-controlled and market-based alternatives. This is because, the survival of the communities living on forest fringes or within forests depend their daily needs on the community forest. However, institutional arrangements evolve along with changes in the structure of political economy. During transitions from common or community property rights regime to private property regime the institutional structures of community-based institution for natural resource management are expected to change as well. The implications of these changes will not be uniform across the different rural classes, primarily because as theoretical and empirical evidences suggest, privatization of commons is often accompanied by increasing inequality in the distribution of resources. The key questions that need to be investigated, in such a context are: Are there any differences in consumption value from community forest between poor and non-poor households? Does the institution-based CPR management results in extraction of more or less forest products? Does this form of forest management improve the welfare of poor households? How do the individual members of the rural community and households change their livelihood strategies in response to these institutional changes?

Arunachal Pradesh, the eastern-most State of North East India, has witnessed large-scale changes in the property rights structure as well as natural resource base. Therefore, community forest offers a unique opportunity to study these enquiries in greater detail. The results are not only expected to clarify the theoretical issues of relationship between Common Property Resource (CPR) management and its distributional aspects in rural settings but also may contribute towards developing a more sophisticated policy responses towards better participatory resource management. In fact, there have been a number of theoretical and empirical studies on the successes and failures of CPR management. However, there are a few studies that have paid attention to equity, equality and its distributional implications of common property institutions as well as rural livelihood strategies.

Hence, the present study is an attempt to fill this gap in knowledge and to highlight some of these aspects, which have been ignored so far.

OBJECTIVES OF THE STUDY

The present study is guided by the following objectives:

(i) To study the degree and nature of forest dependency among the rural households having different asset holding and income or consumption level.

(ii) To analyse the relationship between household's socio-economic characteristics and forest dependency.

(iii) To study the nature of consumption from forest that accrues to the relatively poor and non-poor households and

(iv) To analyse the different sources of livelihood for rural households in the study area.

HYPOTHESES

In the light of the above mentioned objectives, the hypothesis to be tested in the present study are as follows:-

(i) The households belonging to relatively poor group may have a higher dependency over forests in terms of share of consumption generated from forest resources.

(ii) The socio-economic heterogeneity in rural community is expected to determine the different level of consumption from the community forests.

(iii) Access to market may reduce the dependency of households on the community forest since the community members may have some exit options in terms of outside earning opportunities.

METHODOLOGY

The present study is mainly empirical in nature. The data which are used and incorporated in different chapters of the study were collected from primary as well as secondary sources. The State level information has been collected from Arunachal Pradesh Government offices like, Directorate of Economics and Statistics, Directorate of Agriculture, Arunachal Pradesh Remote Sensing and Application Centre, Directorate of Rural Development, Directorate of Environment and Forests and Reports and Publications such as National Sample Survey Organisation, Central Statistical Organisation, Directorate of Census, North Eastern Council, Human Development Report of Arunachal Pradesh, etc. These data have been used for describing the State level picture of CPRs of Arunachal Pradesh. Moreover, the data from the same survey have been incorporated to deal with the general background of the State as well as Lohit and Anjaw districts which are taken up for detailed investigation. In order to complete the district level background such data have been supplemented by information collected from District Office of Economics and Statistics.

In order to have a clear picture of the study area, a location map of Anjaw and Lohit districts of Arunachal Pradesh is shown below in Map 1.1.

Map 1.1: Location Map of Anjaw and Lohit Districrs

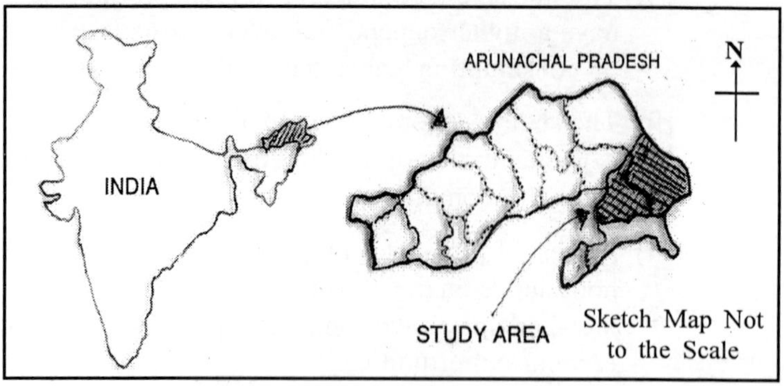

In the field study the preliminary unit of observation is the household of a village. A multi-stage sampling design is used for selection of households of the selected villages. The different stages under the technique are as follows:

Stage I	:	Selection of districts
Stage II	:	Selection of sub-divisions
Stage III	:	Selection of villages
Stage IV	:	Selection of households.

At stage I, two districts namely, Anjaw district and Lohit district were selected by purposive sampling on the basis of forest coverage as well as to represent the two important forms of property rights structure i.e., community and private ownership of forests. At stage II, all the sub-divisions of both the districts i.e., Hayuliang (which is the only sub-division in Anjaw district), Tezu and Namsai (which are the two sub-divisions in the present Lohit district) were considered to represent the entire area. At stage III, seven villages (three villages from Hayuliang sub-division, two villages from Tezu sub-division and four villages from Namsai sub-division) were selected on the basis of purposive sampling. The selected villages from Hayuliang sub-division were Brailiang, Kaniliang and Kasanglat. Danglat and Loiliang were the villages selected from Tezu sub-division and from Namsai sub-division, Chireng, Karhe, Soolungtoo and Tillang Kyong were selected. The details are shown in the Figure 1.1.

The main reasons for selecting the above mentioned villages were based on (i) altitude and (ii) distance of villages from the urban centres i.e., Tezu and Namsai so as to find the degree of dependency on community forest resources. The selection of these villages was taken into consideration on the assumption that the

Fig.:1.1: Design of Sample Survey

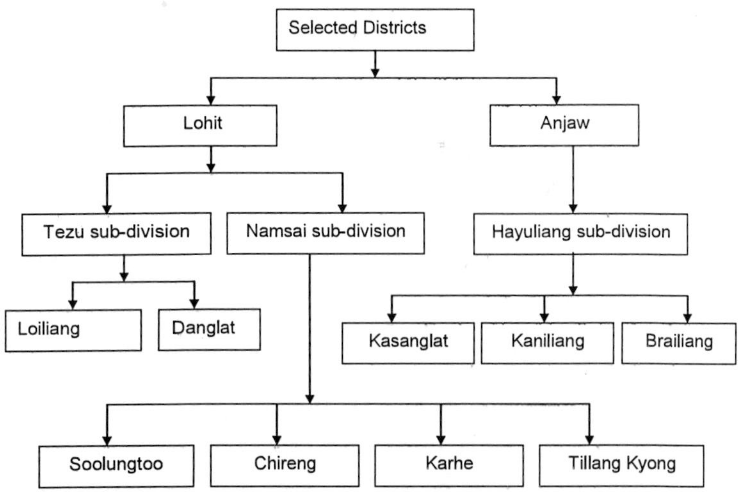

villages nearer to the urban centres may have less dependency on forests because of market access and some exit options in terms of outside earning opportunities in non-farm sector. At the same time, there is also variations of altitude among the surveyed villages. For example, the altitude of Brailiang, Kaniliang and Kasanglat villages are within the range of around 1000-1100 meter above the sea level (the altitude of Goiliang is found at 975 meter above the sea level) and the distance from the nearest urban centre i.e., Tezu is within the range of around 120-128 kilometre. Danglat and Loiliang villages are within the range of around 200-220 meter above the sea level and the distance from Tezu is on an average of 10 kilometre. Soolungtoo village is found at around 140 meter above the sea level and the distance from the nearest urban centre i.e., Namsai is around 10 kilometre. Finally, Chireng, Karhe, and Tillang Kyong villages are found at the range of 680-800 meter above the sea level and the distance from the nearest urban centre i.e., Namsai is within the range of around 17-40 kilometre.

In the next stage, altogether 312 sample households were selected by a stratified random sampling technique of which the total number of surveyed households from Anjaw district stood at 55 sampled households and from Lohit district, it was 257 sampled households. This was done on the basis of proportion of population of both the districts.

These sampled households were further divided into the relatively poor and non-poor households. This was done by compiling a census of village households with Participatory Rural Appraisal (PRA) techniques. The participants in the PRA exercise were asked to categorise all households into two different household groups namely poor and non-poor based on the criteria as to what the villagers consider as important for assessing an individual's socio-economic position in the village. Fox (1983), Richards *et al.*, (1999), and Adhikari (2001) used the similar criteria for categorising households into different groups. This categorisation should be understood in relative terms since all the households in the study area are subsistence *jhumias* and farmers with few households having earning opportunities outside agriculture and CPRs. The sample size consisted of 41.94 per cent of the total households. In small villages all the households were surveyed. In relatively bigger villages like Loiliang, Danglat and Soolungtoo villages of Lohit district, an attempt was made to survey 20 to 35 per cent of the households.

The main tools of the study were two sets of questionnaire namely: (i) household schedule and (ii) village schedule. Both household schedule and village schedule were canvassed in the sampled villages. The household schedule seeks to gather information regarding demography as well as socio-economic characteristics of household, occupational pattern and sources of livelihood, landholdings, tenure and production system, collection and use of forest products from community forest, consumption expenditure and household management system etc. (Annexure X). In case of stock variables, the position on the day of survey was collected, but in case of flow variables, the information of varying periods was taken into account. The data on production, consumption, income etc. were collected for the year preceding the day of survey. On the other hand, the village schedule also seeks to gather information regarding identification of sampled village, village history, availability of infrastructural facilities, particulars of the quality of forests near the village, role of village institutions and institutional framework of resource management and use (Annexure XI). The questionnaires were designed in English for the sake of convenience but were translated into local dialect with the help of interpreters who were part of the survey team at the time of survey wherever necessary. The data collected through the household schedule and village schedule were tabulated in coding sheets to have a clear view of the replies of the respondents and the facts and figures were translated for analytical purposes. Further, the data collected from the field study were also supplemented by the field study notes maintained by the researcher. The details are shown in Table 1.1.

A pilot survey was undertaken in the month of September, 2005. The main field survey however, was initiated in two spells one in the month of December 16, 2005 to January 24, 2006.

In the first spell, the survey team consisted of 4 members from both Lohit and Anjaw districts of Arunachal Pradesh as well as the researcher and the survey of 6 villages namely Brailiang, Danglat, Kaniliang, Kasanglat, Loiliang, Danglat, and Soolungtoo villages was completed.

Table 1.1: Sample Households in the Surveyed Villages of Lohit and Anjaw districts

Name of Village/ District	Altitude (approximate in metres)	Total Number of Households (As per the record of *Gaon Burah* or *Village Chief*)*	Number of Households Surveyed		
			Poor	Non-poor	Total
Kasanglat (Anjaw)	1100	28	17	11	28
Kaniliang (Anjaw)	1050	12	8	4	12
Brailiang (Anjaw)	1000	15	9	6	15
Loiliang (Lohit)	220	327	52	23	75
Danglat (Lohit)	200	165	32	18	50
Soolungtoo (Lohit)	140	105	22	18	40
Chireng (Lohit)	680	12	9	3	12
Karhe (Lohit)	780	56	32	24	56
Tillang Kyong (Lohit)	800	24	15	9	24

Note: *The village level household data for 2001 are not available till date.

It took around 18 days in Anjaw district as the selected villages need to be surveyed by walking onwards on narrow foot tracks from Hayuliang because of the July, 2004 natural calamity (heavy landslides) through which the road communication between Hayuliang and Goiliang was largely snapped. The remaining days were spent in Lohit district for conducting survey.

In the last spell, the survey team also included 3 members, all from the Wakro Circle of the Namsai sub-division in Lohit District and the survey work of Chireng, Karhe and Tillang Kyong villages was covered in the month of November-December, 2006. The researcher also familiarized himself with the study area through staying on posting during August, 1997 to August, 1999 as well as through a detailed analysis of all available secondary information in undivided Lohit district. A number of tables, diagrams and maps were used to facilitate an easy understanding of the subject under consideration. The quantitative and statistical techniques were also incorporated for analytical purposes through an econometric model.

LIMITATIONS OF THE STUDY

There are certain limitations while collecting data in the study area. The limitations which we faced during the survey were mainly due to the problems of measurement and problems of eliciting information which are given below:

(i) There is no traditional standard measure of land, the most important productive asset of rural Arunachal Pradesh.

(ii) Many people in the villages, especially in the remote areas are not well acquainted with the modern quantitative measurements.

For example, in the measurement of agricultural output, the volume and not the standard weights is used. Still today the common practice at the surveyed villages is the measurement of agricultural output such as paddy, millets, maize, soyabean, large cardamom, *kodo*, etc. by baskets while fruits, eatable roots, pumpkin, gourds etc. by numbers and size of the items and firewood by bundles. In case of the domesticated animal like *mithun*, the grabbing system or folding of a rope in the palm which is manually made of thin bamboo chips is encircled in the chest of the animal while measuring its size.

In the study area, the method of measurement in land-use is locally called as dibbling system where a local basket containing approximately 25 to 30 kilograms of millet can plant with a dibble to an area of around 20 *Kathas* or a *Bigha* and 22 *Kathas* are equivalent to an acre of land. On the basis of this information, land-in-use is calculated in hectare. To avoid publicity biases, local academicians and administrators were consulted and necessary rectifications were also made wherever possible.

As a result of these contextual problems, the study is restricted to the use of standard metrology to estimate the variables such as production, income, consumption etc. For example, the estimate of household income in the study area is a complex problem since the production is meant for home consumption and the level of monetisation is very low. Even after intensive survey the income data suffers from a lot of errors. This is because the respondents normally hesitated in reporting his/her income. The level of literacy is very low in the study area. It is not possible to get the reliable income data at the household level. Hence, we have no other alternative but to take a proxy variable of household level consumption value from community forest as well as total consumption expenditure of households. For consumption purpose again edibles, fuels, house building materials etc. gathered from the CPRs which are not marketed and their valuation is a problem. We have taken their imputed value in estimation of consumption. The data on quantities of different items gathered from forests are dependable but the problem is the non-existence of their village level prices. Some of these forest products are, no doubt, locally bartered, but the exchange rate in barter does not reveal the absolute prices which are necessary to arrive at the value. In these circumstances, we used the prices of these products obtaining in the nearest market.

CHAPTER ORGANISATION

The book is organised into seven chapters including the present one, in which the opening statement regarding the background of the study, objectives, hypotheses to be tested, database and methodology as well as limitations and analytical framework have been stated.

The second chapter discusses the literature available on some theoretical issues and approaches to the problems of CPRs management and empirical studies from other countries then to India, in general and the North East and Arunachal Pradesh, in particular.

The third chapter has outlined the property rights structure and the current status of CPRs on the assumptions and concepts used in identifying Common Property Land Resources (CPLR) and Common Property Forest Resources (CPFR) in India and Arunachal Pradesh.

The fourth chapter describes the socio-economic profile of the Arunachal Pradesh in general, the concerned districts and the surveyed villages in particular.

The fifth chapter explores the diverse intricacies of the dependence of rural households on community forest through the econometric model by extensively using statistical techniques.

An attempt is made in the sixth chapter to analyse the CPR management, its distributional implications and the rural livelihood strategies in the surveyed villages of Lohit and Anjaw districts of Arunachal Pradesh.

The last chapter provides the main findings with suggestions and policy implications.

The calculated data along with other related important information including the questionnaires are provided in appendices followed by bibliography.

2

Common Property Resources: Theoretical Formulation with Empirical Evidences

In contemporary economics literature, the term Common Property Resources (CPRs) includes three dimensions which are central to any definition of CPRs: Community, Ownership, and Accessibility. CPRs can be broadly defined as those resources in which a group of people have co-equal use right, specifically formal or legal rights that exclude the use of those resources by other people. CPRs are an important component of the natural resources endowment and the dependence on it to fulfil subsistence needs of rural communities is pronounced. Generally, it may be identified by communal purpose, access and common use. Therefore, it includes the three criteria which are given below:

(i) Ownership pattern of the resource is community-based. The community itself will be well-defined village, subset of people in a village (say tribe or caste based) of a country,

(ii) Indivisible bodies of land, water, air and public spaces where a group larger than a single household or a family unit exercises rights of use and carries responsibility of management, and

(iii) Ownership may be legal or there is a perception of ownership through habitual usage (which is free).

For example, some private land becomes common grazing land through habitual use. It ensures individual access to a resource over which they have collective claim. Members limit their individual claims on a resource in the expectation that other members of the group may do so likewise. Rules of conduct in the use of a given resource are maintained to which all members of the independent group subscribe. In short, it refers to the concept of community resources which have a subtractive but indivisible nature of being a public good.

Many of the eminent academicians have defined it according to their own perception and purview of the study. The eminent among them are Jodha (1990: p. A 65), who described the term common property resources as 'those (non exclusive) resources in which a group whose central purpose is not the use or administration of the resources (*per se*) such as a village, a tribe etc.' The basic elements which Jodha emphasized are 'right to access' by 'a group of people' who are not necessarily the 'owners' of the resources that is used. The examples which Jodha mentioned, in the Indian context, include community pastures, community forest, and waste lands. Later, Pasha (1992: p. 2499) understood the term as those 'resources which are collectively used by a group of people'. The main elements on which he stressed upon are 'resource' having the characteristics of 'collective use' by a group of people. He emphasized the indivisibility nature of the resources which are under the control of a group of individuals but fails to mention the management patterns. Kadekodi (2004: p.19) has defined the term as 'a property on which a well defined collective claims by an exclusive group are established, the use of the resource is subtractive, having the characteristic of a public good such as indivisibility'. The basic elements which he mentioned in the definition include

(i) a group who owns the resource

(ii) subtractive nature of the resource and

(iii) indivisibility of the resource.

Therefore, there is a consensus among the writers on the view which describes CPRs as having three basic elements:

(i) a well-defined group or community having exclusive rights on the use of the resource;

(ii) consumption of the resources are rival and

(iii) the principle of exclusion can not be applied.

COMMON PROPERTY RESOURCES: CONCEPTUAL ISSUES AND EVALUATION

The term CPRs is a concept of recent origin. A number of studies and research works on common property resources management have however, grown in importance and scope since H. Scott Gordon (1954) discussed it in his article 'The Economics of Common Property Resources: The Fishery'. The analysis typically proceeds with the hypothesis that extractors make independent choices with a view to maximizing their material well-being. Since, every individual neglects the implications of his decision on the payoffs of other extractors, this results in sub-optimal level of extraction from the perspective of the group as a whole. He observes that commons can be overexploited when the marginal private cost to an individual is less than the marginal social cost. In other words, over-exploitation of resources starts when marginal private benefit is greater than the marginal social benefit. He demonstrates it academically with an example of ocean fishing by communities. However, the term CPRs which he uses in his study refers to commons i.e., the resources which are open to all or have open access, specifically, water resources, but not land and forest resources.

In pursuance of H. Scott Gordon (1954), a number of studies have been undertaken to elucidate the concept of this terminology whether it has a synonymous application with the terms 'common property resources' and 'commons', 'common property resources' and 'common pool resources', 'common property resources' and 'open access' etc. In order to illuminate these terminologies, a new set of property regimes, like 'Common Pool Property Regime', 'Common Property Regime', and 'Private Property Regime' have set in and the experts have started discussing 'resource use' and 'governance' of the natural resources.

Elinor Ostrom (2000) advances arguments for supplanting the term 'common property' with 'common pool' to avoid this confusion. Common pool resources often have specific characteristics; such as mobility, fluidity, or extensiveness. Therefore, they pose problems to human institutions in respect of their bounding or dividing. However, all common pool resources share two attributes:

(i) it is costly to exclude individuals from using these resources by means of physical barriers or legal instruments, and

(ii) their benefits consumed by one individual are subtracted from the benefits available to others.

Using 'property' in this term to refer to a type of good reinforces the impression that goods sharing these attributes tend to share the same property regime everywhere. But it is not the case (Ostrom, 2000). Hence 'common pool' is not the same as 'common property' (McCay, 1996).

Harold Demsetz (1967) has made an interesting study about the 'ownership patterns' or 'the right of the use of resources'. According to him, private property ownership patterns are superior to community property ownership patterns by virtue of the fact that private property ownership patterns internalize externalities. Taking 'title to land' as an example, he states that two fundamental changes in world economic systems pushed up the privatization of a resource: (i) the rising scarcity of resources due to the population growth and (ii) the rising value of these resources associated with greater market integration and the commercialization of agriculture. As long as there was land abundance and the resource had little commercial value, the marginal cost for existing users of resources compared to an additional user was very small not even worth opposing, and the magnitude of the externalities imposed by each user on extraction by all others was insignificant, making it not worth controlling. As the scarcity and value of resource increases, changing property rights to regulate the entry of private ownership to land would internalize many of the externalities associated with communal ownership, and that an individual owner, vested with ability to exclude other potential users, could realize the rewards and profits emanating from a well-managed property. According to him, a situation where the owners carry both the benefits and the associated costs creates incentives to utilize resources more efficiently. An accompanying argument was that private ownership greatly reduces the costs of negotiating remaining externalities.

However, the process of internalizing the externalities requires a choice between two options. One is to cooperate in the management of CPRs by introducing and enforcing formal rules that deter opportunism in the provision of services to the CPRs and in the appropriation of resources from the CPRs (McCarthy *et.al.*, 2001; Otsuka and Place, 2001). The other is to divide the CPR among the members of the community, either in sub-coalition where cooperation may prevail more easily, or in individual allotments (Baland and Platteau, 1996). The default option prevails when there is a failure to enclose, failure to cooperate in the management of CPRs and failure to enforce individual property rights after division. In this case, incentives to manage the resource for sustained use are missing and there are both under-provision of services of maintenance and over-extraction of the resources, leading to their degradation and depletion.

Arguments in support of private property ownership emerged after Demsetz wrote his paper to reinforce the main claims. Key arguments include greater security of tenure and induced investment, and hence, higher productivity and efficiency, and the potential of private property to function as collateral for loans enabling investments. There is a belief that a secure private tenure curbs degradation by taking externalities into account.

Garrett Hardin (1968), in his article 'The Tragedy of the Commons' has discussed the question of social stability in the light of 'population' and the 'carrying capacity of land'. He opines that if the waiting for the long-desired goal of the social stability becomes a reality, the inherent logic of the commons remorselessly generates tragedy. He argues that people are living in the system that encourages them to increase, as much as possible, the exploitation of limited resources – the situation that leads to ruin for all. Once the resources are open to all, each user attempts to maximize his take without taking the resource conservation, the needs and the benefits of others into account. Hardin further argues that the solutions to the problems of resource depletion and degradation are not technical but rather lie in governmental control and regulation of resource use. So he suggests privatization as an optimal solution capable of avoiding the ruin for all (Berkes *et al.*, 1989, pp. 91-93). To explain how the tragedy would occur, he says, "A rational herdsman concludes that the only sensible course for him to pursue is to add another animal to his herd and another. … But this is the conclusion reached by each and every rational herdsman sharing a commons. Therein is the tragedy. Each man is locked into a system that compels him to increase his herd without limit - in a world that is limited. Ruin is the destination towards which all men rush, each pursuing his own best interest in a society that believes in the freedom of the commons. Freedom in a commons brings ruin to all". (Hardin, 1968, p. 1244).

Gordon (1954), Demsetz (1967), Hardin (1968) and others have discussed the most efficient institutional management of sustainable resource use and conservation of natural resources. It has been argued that in case of open-access and unregulated common property, individuals do not get proper incentive to act in socially efficient way and hence the 'tragedy of commons' occurs (Hardin, 1968). But they blurred the distinction between open access and common property resources until Ciriacy-Wantrup and Bishop (1975: p. 714), presented a clear exposition of 'common property as a social institution' in which property ownership patterns in resources are distributed among a number of owners who are 'co-equals in their rights to use the resources'. Ciriacy-Wantrup and Bishop, (1975) are critical to the view placed by Hardin. They argue that the term 'commons' in the 'tragedy of commons' is applicable to the situation of appropriation of 'open access resources' and not to 'common property resources'. In support to their argument, it has been stated that in case of open-access and unregulated common property resources, individuals do not get proper incentive to act in socially efficient way and hence the 'tragedy of commons' occurs. In common property resources, all group members (community or interest group) have equal rights to use the resource and to exclude non-group members (Ciriacy-Wantrup and Bishop, 1975), and have to regulate this use and invest in conservation. One of the objectives for excluding non-members is to avoid overexploitation of the resources without contributing to its management and conservation (McKean and Ostrom, 1995).

According to Berkes *et al.*, (1989), Hardin defends the divergence between the individual and the collective rationality in resource use without considering the auto-regulation capacity of the users. In addition, he assumes that persons are unable to limit access and institute rules that regulate use without governmental control or privatization (Berkes *et al.*, 1989; Feeny *et al.*, 1990). In many parts of the world, Hardin's arguments were used to nationalize and privatize natural resources which strengthened top-down planning and development approaches, ignoring local institutions (Arnold and Campbell, 1986) resulting into undesirable social and environmental impacts.

Other solutions exist in addition to those proposed by Hardin because the government control or privatization has no success in some situations (Hanna *et al.*, 1996; Ostrom *et al.*, 1999). For example, a large appropriation of renewable and non-renewable resources by national and international capital in some regions of Brazilian Amazon, has led to an unprecedented depletion of natural resources and the marginalization of local populations (Diegues, 2000:p. 8).

Hardin's theory confounds CPRs and free access - the absence of property rights and a situation where rights and duties are not well defined (McKean and Ostrom, 1995; McCay, 1996) leading to overexploitation. By equating common property ownership patterns with free access and assuming that free access leads to overexploitation, Hardin's theory equates common property resources management with overexploitation (McCay and Acherson, 1987; Berkes *et al.*, 1989). On the other hand, the theory assumes that individual interests are incompatible with existent management institutions but, in many communities, natural resource users are driven by social pressure to be in conformity with enforcement rules and conducts prescribed (Mc Cay, 1996).

More recent elaborations are found in Bromley (1989a, 1989b, 1991), McCay and Acheson (1987), Bromley and Cernea (1989), and Larson and Bromley (1990). These studies discuss the resource use and the governance of the natural resources through diverse constellations of institutions - rights, rules, and conventions—that are enforced externally by a legitimate source of coercion, or internally by the actions of the resource users themselves. They differentiate one fundamental difference between an 'open-access' and 'CPRs' is that CPRs has a 'boundary' that distinguishes between the 'owners' and 'non-owners' of particular benefit streams generated by collectively-used natural resources. Both the corporate model of common property and the coordination model of common property assume that there is a recognized group of resource owners whose rights to access and utilize particular resource benefit streams are protected by a legitimate unit of coercion that has the power to prevent encroachment by non-members. This structure provides the common property resources with the external legitimacy needed to differentiate it from an open-access resource. The corporate model, as presented by Dasgupta and Heal (1979) and Dorfman (1974) assumes that the co-owners of the resources are able to devise explicit mechanisms for enforcing rules on resource access and allocation. The coordination model, or assurance model, offered by Runge (1981, 1986) proposes that there are certain conditions under which self-enforcing institutions are sufficient to support mutually-beneficial resource use. He argues that these models are somewhat narrow and must be modified somewhat in their application to a traditional context but this argument fails to account for the fluidity of the institutions, the governance structures, the production techniques, as well as the environmental conditions that characterize those pastoral regimes.

Opinions enunciated by economics and other social sciences are divided in respect of the terminologies of 'property' and 'commons'. The proposition relating to the understanding of institutions and their management, particularly, governance and policy processes from local to global remains a matter of controversy. Thus, there emerge three different schools of thought in the literature of common property of land and forest: common property rights, private property rights, and state property rights. It has been observed that they avert the tragedy of commons in respect of the institutional arrangements of the natural resources. The scholars of the first school of thought emphasize on the institution building at the local level for managing common pool resources as the state managed natural resources often degraded faster. It is also mentioned that state pool resources were used inefficiently as a result of which the outcome was not beneficial to the poor. As an alternative to both the market and the state-controlled institutional arrangements, local level decentralized management of CPRs has been highlighted (Baland and Platteau, 1996; Ostrom, 2000). Ostrom argues that collective action for CPR management will be long enduring and successful under the conditions of well-defined boundaries, congruence between appropriation and provision rules, effective monitoring, graduated sanctions, conflict-resolution mechanisms and minimal recognition of rights to organize (Ostrom, 1990). Common property rights constitute a form of private property (McKean and Ostrom, 1995) because community members or members within an interest group are co-owners of the resource and have the right to exclude others from use of the resources. In essence, there is a privatization of access and use rights by a group without dividing the resources in parts.

According to the second property rights school, the problem of overexploitation and degradation of commons can be solved only by creating and enforcing private property rights (Demsetz, 1967; Cheung, 1970). It argues that common property regimes are inefficient because of three reasons: (i) rent dissipation i.e., no one owns the products of the resource until they are captured, and everyone engages in an unproductive race to capture these products before others do (Gordon, 1954; Cheung, 1970), (ii) high transaction and enforcement costs. There is possibility of high transaction and enforcement costs if communal owners try to devise rules to reduce the externalities of their mutual overuse (Demsetz, 1967; Coase, 1960) and (iii) low productivity. Production tends to become low since no one has an incentive to invest in order to increase his private returns (North, 1990). Thus, private property is considered the most efficient way to internalize the externalities generated from the overexploitation and degradation of the commons. It also makes the contention that private property rights spontaneously emerge to increase efficiency (Demsetz, 1967 and Posner, 1977).

The third school advocates that most of the crucial assumptions of the property rights school, such as zero enforcement costs, well-defined property rights, competitive and efficient markets, are non-existent in reality and hence privatization may not be an effective solution to the problem of resource use. In practice, such conditions are absent for commons since non-divisibility of the resources violates the assumptions of the property right school. Moreover, distributional implication of privatization may not be socially desirable (Weitzman, 1974). Hardin says that only the allocation of full authority to regulate the commons to external agency i.e., state property regime could reduce the overexploitation of commons.

It is useful in this regard to employ Agrawal's (2001) synthesis of major research findings related to common property regimes. He has looked particularly into Wade's, Ostrom's, and Baland and Platteau's work, and what he has found is that many of the enabling factors, such as resource characteristics, group characteristics, institutional arrangement and external environment in determining the viability of institutions for the commons that the authors have arrived at, overlap—although there are some discrepancies.

Therefore, much of the research on common property resource management has centered on identifying the conditions under which such systems thrive and has consequently given rise to two major lines of arguments. Two conditions must be fulfilled in order to enable the common property management systems to function - one is a clear demarcation of physical boundaries of resources and the other is the presence of unambiguous social boundaries, i.e. group membership must be in place for common property arrangements to work. The property rights school argues that private property is the most appropriate way to internalize the externalities that are generated in the former cases. It also makes the contention that private property rights will spontaneously emerge to increase efficiency (Demsetz, 1967 and Posner, 1977).

COLLECTIVE ACTION AND PARTICIPATION

Collective action and participation in natural resource management arise because of heavy state involvement, prevalence of market failures (such as positive and negative externalities) and the strategic importance of the resources. The term 'collective action' is an amalgamated institution of three sectors of natural resource management: (i) the private sector, (ii) the collective action sector, and (iii) the public sector. These three sectors differ, among other things, by the assignment of property rights and the incentives of compliance which make people cooperate through appreciation, influence, consummation, action and evaluation. Property rights in private sector are assigned to individual's utility maximization with the primary incentive for cooperation. In the collective action sector, responsibility is allotted to a group of people where cooperation is based on normative-voluntary incentives. But in the public sector, it is assigned to the state where cooperation is enforced with sanctions and penalties as the primary incentives. The different management sectors can also be perceived as a continuum with the private sector on the one end and the public sector on the other. In between these two opposite points, we find the collective action sector in which local-level organizations provide resource management (Uphoff, 1993: pp. 612-614).

The term 'participation' refers to the process of involvement by an economic agent in any development activity. Some researchers define the nature and context of participation as organization with new rules, regulations and institutions (Pearse, 1998) and others describe, it as empowering people in decision-making, project implementation and sharing benefits (Uphoff, 1986; Paul, 1989).

There have been an increasing number of empirical studies of user-managed resource systems since 1970s which suggest that state-managed natural resources were often degraded faster and used inefficiently and the outcome was not necessarily beneficial to the poor. Thus, state-managed natural resources were not the only or even always the best option. Since the mid 1980s there has been greater attention to local-level decentralized management of CPRs in the theoretical literature (Runge, 1986; Ostrom *et al.*, 1990; Bromley, 1992; Prakash and Gupta, 1997). These studies have highlighted local level decentralized management of CPRs as an alternative to both market and state controlled institutional arrangements. They have also argued that collective action for CPR management does not necessarily lead to a 'tragedy of common' provided there are effective systems of local-level decentralized management of CPRs.

The factors identified in collective action and participation in the natural resource management can be divided into three criteria:

(i) physical and technical characteristics of the resource;

(ii) characteristics of the group of resource users; and

(iii) attributes of institutional arrangements.

The first criterion stresses on distinguishing the type of resource on the basis of the degree of excludability and subtractability or rivalry of the resources. Excludability relates to the cost of preventing others from using the resource, while subtractability refers to situations in which use of resource by an individual reduces the amount of resources available to others. Resources which have high excludability but also high subtractability can be managed efficiently as private property; those with low excludability as well as low subtractability are public goods which the state can provide; and those with low excludability and high subtractability are common property resources which are most prone to degradation through the 'tragedy of commons' if resource management entities are lacking. Excludability and subtractability in turn are influenced by the size of the resource system and the natural boundness of the resource (Ostrom, 1992: pp.295-96).

The second criterion emphasizes specifically on the number of resource users. The smaller the group, the more homogeneous is likely to be the interest of the resource users (Bardhan, 1993; Ostrom, 1990; Bromely, 1992). It is stated that with an increasing number of resource users, the possibility of local-level decentralized management of CPRs decreases. To support the argument, the degree of homogeneity becomes an intermediate variable between the size of the group and the degree of organization. This intermediate variable is positively linked to the dependent variable. In natural resource management context, there is similarity in resource access and perceptions of the risk of the long-term resource exploitation. Moreover, consistency in norms, in general, has been identified as the crucial factor affecting the possibility of collective action and participation and the degree of organization (Bardhan, 1993; Ostrom, 1990). Therefore, heterogeneity in resource asset structure can lead to possibility of local-level decentralized management of CPRs (Ostrom, 1992). Openness and stability of the community is another crucial determinant of the possibility of collective action and participation. The higher the rate of migration, mobility and market integration, the lower is the possibility of collective action and participation (Baland and Platteau, 1996; Bardhan, 1993; Ostrom, 1986; 1990).

Finally, the last criterion stresses on the attributes of institutional arrangements. There are three levels of institutional arrangements: (i) operational rules, (ii) collective choice rules, and (iii) constitutional rules. The operational rules of natural resource management directly affect the use of the resource in terms of who can participate, what the participant may, must and must not do and how they are rewarded and punished. They can be either formal or informal rules which include the following five categories of operational rules for the collective action and participation at local-level decentralized management of CPRs. They are: (i) well-defined boundary and access rules defining the resource system in terms of area and members, (ii) congruence between appropriation and provision rules defining who is getting what, (iii) input rules explaining in what way the users contribute, (iv) penalty rules well-marking the effective monitoring and sanctions, and (v) conflict resolution rules or mechanisms. Ostrom claims that collective action for CPR management will be long enduring and successful under conditions of well defined boundaries, congruence between appropriation and provision rules, effective monitoring, graduated sanctions, conflict-resolution mechanisms and minimal recognition of rights to organize (Ostrom, 1986; 1990).

The collective choice rules give guidelines for formulating and enforcing or changing operational rules (Tang, 1992). These rules define who is eligible and how the future operational rules will be regulated (Ostrom, 1990: pp.141-42). The extent of participation of the resource users affected by the operational rules has been emphasized as a crucial factor at this level of institutional arrangements.

The constitutional rules refer to the external arrangements such as any public regulation of relevance. Local-level decentralized management of CPRs becomes easier when the arrangements in the external environment are supporting the process.

Another important aspect of collective action and participation about whether or not resource users are capable of cooperation is found in the game theory (Bardhan, 1993: p.634; Feeny, *et al.*, 1990: pp.1-3; Ostrom, 1990: pp.2-14; Baland and Platteau, 1996). The choice which the resource user confronts is also viewed as a comparison of expected benefits and costs of alternative choices of actions with economic concepts of cost and benefits. After the classical Prisoner's Dilemma Game, the application of the game theory in natural resource management leads to more optimistic views. These games take into account the interactions between individuals. The major game theories which are used in natural resource managements are: Chicken Game, Assurance Game, Repeated Prisoner's Dilemma Game with tit-for-tat strategy, and Fairness Game. The Chicken Game is the simplest of the four. It describes one-shot situation in which at least either of the players will cooperate because both the players like to avoid a dominant strategy of defection. The Assurance Game is the coordination game where the payoff structure the players face is not as favourable as in the Chicken Game. Either player prefers symmetric solutions. Accordingly there is no dominant strategy. Thus, communication between the players is crucial for collective action and participation. The Repeated Prisoner's Dilemma Game is the game of cooperation. If cooperation gets started it will be reciprocated as either player plays whatever the previous player played. The argument is that each player accumulates experience of the behaviour of his opponent and is able to recall his past moves (Baland and Platteau, 1996). The Fairness Game is also another strategy of cooperation game. The argument is that the players will not hesitate to cooperate because they know that if they do so the other player will follow suit.

DESIGN PRINCIPLES FOR SUCCESSFUL COLLECTIVE ACTION

The success or failure of any property rights structure to protect natural resources is more a feature of the ability to regulate access and use of the property than whether the property is private, commons or state property (Feeny *et al.*, 1990). Ostrom (1986; 1990) proposes eight principles for successful collection action found in studying common property management regimes. These principles include:

(i) Clearly defined boundaries of access and use

(ii) Relevance of rules to local resource conditions

(iii) Collective choice arrangement for decision making

(iv) Effective monitoring of access and uses of the CPR

(v) Graduated sanctions for violators of rules

(vi) Conflict resolution mechanisms

(vii) Minimal recognition of rights to organize by external authorities

(viii) Nested management of larger common property systems.

These principles expand the attributes of CPR management including self-government at the local level of a commonly used resource in a way to exclude outsiders, and involve the recognition, monitoring and enforcing rules to use the common resource.

Ostrom's work strongly influenced subsequent works on CPRs. Ostrom's framework has been used in both theoretical and empirical research on the commons to extend her analysis. In fact, the level of design principles identified by her has been further extended by later scholars. Table 2.1 gives an overview of these principles.

Table: 2.1: Design Principles for Successful Collective Action

	Wade's Condition for Successful CPR Management (1987)
i)	Nature of the resource
ii)	Costs of exclusion technology
iii)	Relationship between resources and user groups
iv)	Characteristics if user groups
v)	Notice ability of cheating
vi)	Relationship between user and State
	Hanna, Folk & Maler's Design Principles of Property Rights Regimes (1996)
i)	Definition of legitimate interests in the CPRs
ii)	Articulation of rules for user participation
iii)	Congruence of rights and responsibilities
iv)	Incentive structure of rules reflect long run sustainability of CPRs
v)	Congruence of boundaries
vi)	Distribution of decision making boundaries
vii)	Provisioning of monitoring, sanction and enforcement mechanism
	Pinkerton and Weinstein's Basic Criteria for Fruitful Collective Action (1995)
i)	Accountability
ii)	Effectiveness
iii)	Representativeness
iv)	Adaptability

Source: Edwards, V. M. and N. A. Steins (1998), p.16.

BEYOND DESIGN PRINCIPLES: CONTEXTUAL FACTORS

Steins, Edwards and Rolling (2000) have argued that there are many problems related to design principles. The most important is that CPR school has focused on studying the workings of the commons from the view point of the resource of the community. There has been no attempt to take a view of the commons from the view point located outside the community i.e., CPR theory has not attempted to link the collective action arena to the external wall. Thus, the CPR theorists ignored the role of contextual factors—dynamic remote factors outside the control of the community.

In recent years, the socio-economic change has led to the interrelated changes. These are as follows:

(i) rapid demographic expansion;

(ii) the destruction of the self-sufficiency of the local communities;

(iii) an erosion of traditional sanctioning forces based upon norms and social ties;

(iv) the interlinking of the formulating isolated local communities with the national economy;

(v) an increase in the importance of commercial forces in the functioning of the local economies; and

(vi) the spreading of centralized political authorities to local communities.

Result of these changes is that the Cost-Benefit Analysis of institutional provisioning is being increasingly affected by factors that are external to the community which lie outside the control. Such factors are not only determining the success of the regime at a particular point of time, but also affecting the dynamics of the institutional changes. The increase in importance of such factors necessitates that inclusion into an analysis of the creating and functioning of the CPR regime. These in turn, call for a modification of the traditional framework of the analysis.

STUDIES OF CPRs IN INDIA

Consistent with the growing theoretical issues, there are enough empirical studies with regional variations in India dealing with common property and community-based natural resource management. Campbell, J.G. (1980) in his study on the issues of forestry in Madhya Pradesh found that a large percentage of rural poor has usufruct rights on state land. Revenue lands are freely available for unlimited grazing unless claimed by the Government or Panchayat (local council) for some particular project. Traditional access rights (*nistar*) give unlimited grazing and minor forest collection rights to rural residents in forests classified as protected and even in the remaining forests classified as reserved. The government reserves to itself the right of cutting any of the most valuable tree and bamboo species existing on private lands. Management of public lands almost exclusively consists in protecting the division of harvesting rights within the same lands between the government and the people. There is a high degree of ambiguity about the ownership rights on uncultivated revenue land, illegally occupied revenue land and illegally operated forest land.

Basu, N.G. (1984) in his case study on the importance of non-governmental or private voluntary organizations (NGOs, PVOs) in the successful development of community forestry in Bihar had found that some 120 villages there are inhabited mostly by tribal people, where deforestation has reduced the land still under forest to 12-15 per cent. Some villages have independently initiated schemes for protecting and developing the remaining natural forest. The catalytic role of local NGOs in stimulating further development of communal forest management is noted.

Shiva, V. (1986) in his study on CPRs management observed that the government action to privatize common land accentuates rural poverty and increases ecological instability. Only a few marginal and landless farmers will gain at the cost of the majority who derive a wealth of benefits from these lands. Singh, Ch. (1986) considered the exact legal position concerning the current rights of forest-dwellers in India and ascertained what could be done for them in future legislation. Further he observed that most rural Indians depend on CPRs for their energy and housing needs; the dependency being the greatest in tribal areas. One conclusion is that the Indian Forest Lands Acts should be repealed and that new acts should be created, in order to reach a point of equal distribution and use of natural resources.

Ballabh, V. and Singh, K. (1988) in their study of institutions of forest management in Uttar Pradesh had found that Forest Councils have the authority to levy fines for misuse of forest resources and collect fees from users. They are responsible for internal management and grazing, the collection of fuelwood, fodder and for protection. Forest Council members are informally elected and produce is distributed fairly among the members of the village community. Although the authority to levy fees and fines and to punish offenders has been reduced because of rule changes, this method of forest management is considered promising.

Brokensha, D. (1988) discussed CPRs and considered a wide range of socio-economic and biophysical factors. The common lands of Karnataka include *gomal* lands, tank foreshores and "wastelands". Most common lands are degraded. He observed that CPRs cannot be examined in isolation. Without participation in decision-making and management of social forestry projects there is no social forestry.

Arnold, J.E.M. and Stewart, W.C. (1989) in their study in social forestry in Tamil Nadu had observed that conflicts over the use of CPRs were handled too easily, and the complexities of changing use of the common lands and resources were over-estimated. The study has found that in the 19th century, up to two thirds of the land in India was under community control but privatization and government appropriation have reduced this share. Many traditional and indigenous forms of CPRs management have weakened or collapsed. They observed that, despite the erosion of CPRs, they still play a very important role in agricultural systems and in the livelihoods of the poor. In order to make progress towards sustainable CPRs management it will be necessary to give high priority to correcting policy, legal anomalies, and weaknesses which undermine CPRs management arrangements or which encourage further privatization.

Iyengar, S. (1989), in his case study in 25 villages located in five different geo-physical regions in Gujarat found that the development of infrastructure facilities, such as roads and transport networks, has opened up markets for some natural resources. While this is a healthy development, it has also resulted in far too rapid growth in the rate of exploitation of the resources. Since independence, the population, including that of rural areas, has grown at a very rapid rate. This has increased pressure on available land. The area under CPR land in villages has decreased and continues to do so because of privatization. Over-use and over-exploitation of land has also led to deterioration in its quality. As a result, the status and area of CPR land has changed considerably.

On the present status of the management of CPRs such as water, grazing lands and forests, Chopra *et al.*, (1989) in their study of participatory management of CPRs in Haryana had observed that the strategy to control the degradation of CPRs lies on (i) a group of people, (ii) adherence to certain set of rules, customs, tradition, and (iii) empowerment and adjustments between individual behaviour and group behaviour. They argued that the intervention of government in the management of CPRs led to excessive overexploitation of the resource.

Jodha, N.S. (1986; 1987; 1990) analysed the extent of the dependence of various user groups on these CPRs and their management characteristics. According to him, the decline in CPR area, as well as the physical degradation and deterioration of the management arrangements is caused by effects of public interventions, commercialization, technological change and demographic factors. The demographic factors which he mentioned are (i) physical loss of the natural resource system (due to submersion of grazing land in a newly constructed dam or area of CPR covered by roads and buildings) (ii) deterioration of physical productivity of resources (such as degradation of pastures and forest lands) and (iii) reassignment of usage and property rights as indicated by transfer of CPR lands to private ownership. Rich and poor people respond in different ways to the changing status of the CPRs. While rich people tend to withdraw from CPR use and increasingly rely on alternative land use options (including CPR privatization), the poor tend to continue to rely on CPRs for sustenance; they attempt to maximize the complementary relations between CPRs and private resources. Although there are various factors constraining the present and future management and proper utilization of CPRs, there are three important reasons to improve prospects for future CPRs management: ecological imperatives to keep fragile lands under low-intensity use, the complementary nature of CPRs to private property resources, and sustenance of the rural poor who lack alternative options for resource utilization. Factors to consider in strengthening CPRs management are positive CPRs policies, increased productivity through higher investments and new technology, improved management regulations and formation of well-defined user groups. He also attempted to quantify the extent to which the rural poor benefit from CPRs, based on data from over 80 villages in 21 districts of Western dryland states. The study reveals the significant contribution of CPRs towards the employment and income generation of the rural poor; i.e., labour and small farm households. Despite the contributions of CPRs, their area and productivity are declining in all of the regions. Large scale privatization of CPRs has taken place during the last three decades, in an effort to help the poor. He further, perceived that the privatization of CPRs as a strategy to help rural poor yielded a negative results and also reduce the productivity of the commons. The 49 per cent to 86 per cent of the privatized CPRs ended up in the hands of non-poor. Furthermore, most of the land received by the poor households was also given up by them because they did not have complementary resources with which to develop and use it. He calls for greater attention to CPRs as a part of the anti-poverty strategy.

Chen, M. (1991) in his study of a single village of 59 poor households in Ahmedabad district of Gujarat also found that conflict over privatization of CPRs increases over time. Pasha, S. A. (1992) in his study of 14 villages in Karnataka observed that community-based use and management of CPRs with the active participation of all the rural households is an essential factor for protection of these resources. Similarly, Beck, T. (1994) in his study of three villages in West Bengal observed that conflicts over CPRs are central to poor household's experience of poverty. On the similar lines, Singh, *et al.*, (1996) in their study of eight villages in Punjab also found that the main factors for the decline of CPRs were the mismanagement and encroachment problems. Thus, the authors stressed on the need for effective people's participation in preventing over exploitation of CPRs by the better off households and in protecting the forests in particular.

Most of these literatures emphasized efficient collective action and participation in CPRs management system so as to ensure equity and sustainability of resource management at the local level.

STUDIES OF CPRs IN NORTH-EAST INDIA AND ARUNACHAL PRADESH

In spite of the fact that almost all the states of North East India have a good percentage of area under CPRs, but very few studies have been carried to date regarding the forest dependency and management of CPRs in the region in general, and Arunachal Pradesh in particular. The studies of Roy and Kuri (1997) had tried to show the process of change of property rights in Arunachal Pradesh through the identification of the factors involved in the process. Das (1995) studied the transition of communal ownership of land to its individualization. Ganguly (1997) showed for North East in general and Arunachal Pradesh in particular that there were growing inequalities in the *jhum*-based economy which was due to the emergence of private property rights in land. Priyanka (2004) observed that the establishment of property rights in land inequalities in Arunachal Pradesh but the relationship between property rights and production efficiency was not very statistically significant. Nevertheless, the binary comparisons in her study between '*jhum* farms and permanent agricultural farms' as well as 'share-cropped farms and owned-cultivated farms' were found to have a positive relationship between the degree of property rights and efficiency in production.

The above studies suffer from certain shortcomings particularly in the management of CPRs and its distributional implications in livelihood strategies of the rural stakeholders. These studies have concentrated mainly on the issues of property rights of land only. Only few studies have been conducted recently (Mitra, 1998; 2003; Mitra and Mishra, 2005) regarding the common property forest resources and institutional structures for forest resource management. Hence, the present study is an attempt to fill in this gap in knowledge in dealing with common property forest resources, forest dependency, its distributional implications as well as changing livelihood strategies of the people of the two eastern-most districts of the Country.

3

Common Property Resources and Property Rights in India and Arunachal Pradesh

The review of the available literature in the preceding chapter reveals that the use, status and management procedures of CPRs have strong regional variations. Therefore, in order to come to any conclusion, it is essential to analyse the causes of these regional variations in-depth. Hence, this chapter is devoted to the study of the dimensions of CPRs in India and its regional variations during the last three decades. The analysis is based on the data collected from the secondary sources like different government publications and official websites. Further, in the analysis, the concept of land resources has been used which is broadly classified as land and forests for their dimensionality.

STATUS OF CPRs IN INDIA

The communities all over India had an access to several types of commons, by tradition or through formal and informal conventions. There are no official estimates about the status of CPRs in India. However, several attempts have been made by different academicians based on different methodologies. Studies in CPRs in India both from the policy and the research perspectives date back to mid-1980s. In terms of assessing the status of such resources, Jodha's seminal work (1986) remains the most extensive village-level analysis which studies the magnitude of common property land resources in the dry land of the Western Region of the country. Besides Jodha, a number of micro-level assessments have also been conducted subsequently. After the publication of the 54th Round of National Sample Survey Organisation (NSSO) data (1999) on the current status of CPRs in India, researchers began to have an access to it. The NSSO data is unique in the sense that it is based on the study of 78,990 rural households in 5114 villages making it a comprehensive countrywide study of CPRs. However, there are reasons to believe that the enumeration process of such a rapid survey is likely to be less accurate than in-depth long term ethnographic field research. For example, if illegality is involved in the use of some types of CPRs, respondents may be unwilling to reveal it to the enumerators who do not know the truth. Chopra and Gulati (1990) uses Agricultural Land Use Statistics data to quantify the magnitude of common property land and forest resources in the 1970s at all India level. This was followed by a study of Suresh Kumar (2000) and Kadekodi (2001). Kadekodi (2001) estimates the extent of the resources by using CMIE and Land Utilisation Statistics.

Another problem is the methodological approach of exclusion and inclusion of the resource on the basis of *'de jure'* or *'de facto'* methods. Chopra and Gulati (1990) and Kadekodi (2001) calculate CPRs as the sum total of 'private land' to which common access may exist viz., 'cultivable waste land', 'fallows other than current fallows', 'permanent pastures and grazing land', 'barren and uncultivable land', and 'protected' and 'unclassed forests'. NSSO (1999) uses the *de jure* approach and excludes forest areas. Despite these obvious limitations, the data provides a very useful baseline against the measurement of the extent and the degree of CPRs. Thus, all the studies provide a rough estimation of CPRs across the country, based on a reclassification of land use data. Table 3.1 shows the alternative estimates of CPRs provided by different academicians and organization.

Table 3.1: Alternative Estimates of CPRs in Different States of India

(in per cent)

State	Jodha -1986	Chopra & Gulati (1990)	NSSO (1999)	Kadekodi (2001)
Andhra Pradesh	11	16	9	23
Assam	-	-	7	25
Bihar	-	30	8	31
Gujarat	11	17	27	17
Haryana	-	4	3	4
Himachal Pradesh	-	93	12	90
Jammu & Kaskmir	-	1.2	-	2
Karnataka	16	17	10	19
Kerala	-	8	-	8
Madhya Pradesh	24	32	22	32
Maharashtra	15	26	11	23
Meghalaya	-	-	-	70
Nagaland	-	-	8	53
Orissa	-	31	11	29
Punjab	-	7	1	7
Rajasthan	14	35	32	42
Sikkim	-	-	14	-
Tamil Nadu	10	21	12	19
Tripura	-	-	1	30
Uttar Pradesh	-	13	12	9
West Bengal	-	7	2	7

Source: Different Works of Different Academicians and Organisations.

Table 3.1 shows the large variations of the extent of CPRs in various States of India which is mainly due to different concepts and methodology used in the estimation procedure.

Let us first discuss the methodology of arriving at the estimates of 'Common Property Land Resources' (CPRL) and 'Common Property Forest Resources' (CPRF). The 'CPRL' refers to the land identified with a common user's right, specifically by rural community. It includes 'barren and uncultivable land' (BUL), 'permanent pastures and grazing land' (PPGL), 'cultivable wasteland' (CWL), and 'fallows other than current fallows' (OTCF). Similarly, the 'CPRF' is the subset of total reported forest area minus reserve forests to which common property rights are assumed to exist. It includes 'protected forest land' and 'unclassified forest land'. Table 3.2 presents the land categories, assumptions and concepts used in identifying CPRL and CPRF in India.

Table 3.2: Identification of Common Property Resources

Classification of land	Included in CPRs?	Source of sanction for access (as assumed in the estimation)
Net sown area	No	On uncultivated owned land: limited user rights
Current fallow	No	On uncultivated owned land: limited user rights
Fallow other than current	Yes	User rights by convention
Cultivable waste	Yes	Partial user rights by convention
Pastures and other grazing land	Yes	User rights by law
Barren and uncultivable land	May be included	No access
Area put to non-agricultural use	May be included	No access
Forest area		
1. Reserved	No	No access
2. Protected	Partial	Partial user rights
3. Unclassed	Yes	User rights by law

Source: Kadekodi, G. K., *Common Property Resource Management*, Oxford, 2004.

The 'BUL' is the area which is not available for cultivation. Therefore, it may be included in 'CPRL'. Such land is covered by roads, buildings, water, mountains, railways, deserts and others which are otherwise appropriated for non-agricultural purposes. The 'OTCF' has common user rights by convention while partial use rights exist on the 'CWL'. However the 'PPGL' has common user rights by law. On the other hand, unclassified forests, with very low productivity, are always open to use by local communities. Accordingly, a part of 'CPRF', keeping in mind that this may yield an over-estimate of land to which common access may exit. Therefore, an attempt has been made to estimate of 'CPRL' and 'CPRF' for the year 2001 for different states of India including the State of Arunachal Pradesh and Union Territories.

For convenience, the CPRs have been categorized under four classes:

(i) Very high (75 per cent and above);

(ii) High (50-75 per cent);

(iii) Medium (25-50 per cent); and

(iv) Low (below 25 per cent).

Table 3.3 provides the composition of CPR area across different states including Arunachal Pradesh and Union Territories of India during 2001.

The estimation as mentioned in Table 3.3 can be described under four categories:

(i) The states which fall under the category of 'very high' level of CPRs of the total area are Manipur (88.00), and Himachal Pradesh (82.81). On account of being hilly regions, these states show varying characteristics of CPRs. This is because of large areas of protected forests which decreases CPRL to an unusual low level.

(ii) Interestingly, the extent of CPRs available between the range of 50 - 75 per cent for the states *viz.*, Meghalaya (70.31) Nagaland (58.87), Mizoram (57.02) and Arunachal Pradesh (52.06 per cent) respectively. The higher extent

Table 3.3: Composition of CPR Area across Different States and Union Territories of India during 2001

('000 hectare)

State/UT	Geographical Area	BUL	PPGL	CWL	OTCF	CPRL	CPRF	CPRs	% of CPRs to total area
Andhra Pradesh	27507	2100	675	728	1417	4920	1334	6254	22.74
Arunachal Pradesh	8374	21	4	37	46	108	4251	4359	52.06
Assam	7844	1461	163	80	65	1769	895	2664	33.96
Bihar	17388	1010	105	321	922	2358	2460	4818	27.71
Goa	370	0	1	55	0	56	49	105	28.39
Gujarat	19602	2604	849	1982	13	5448	507	5955	30.38
Haryana	4421	102	34	19	0	155	130	285	6.45
Himachal Pradesh	5567	807	153	124	13	1097	3513	4610	82.81
Jammu & Kashmir	22224	291	126	140	8	565	0	565	2.54
Karnataka	19179	794	959	427	409	2589	1010	3599	18.77
Kerala	3886	29	0	59	34	122	18	140	3.60
Madhya Pradesh	44344	1349	1585	1201	575	4710	7179	11889	26.81
Maharashtra	30771	1696	1341	903	1171	5111	1270	6381	20.74
Manipur	2233	0	0	0	370	370	1595	1965	88.00

Meghalaya	2243	136	0	441	162	739	838	1577	70.31
Mizoram	2108	16	23	127	156	322	880	1202	57.02
Nagaland	1658	0	0	65	79	144	832	976	58.87
Orissa	15571	843	443	392	430	2108	3178	5286	33.95
Punjab	5036	55	7	25	4	91	301	392	7.78
Rajasthan	34224	2566	1707	4908	2444	11625	2063	13688	40.00
Sikkim	710	173	69	1	9	252	39	291	40.99
Tamil Nadu	13006	476	123	352	1228	2179	355	2534	19.48
Tripura	1049	3	0	1	1	5	270	275	26.22
Uttar Pradesh	29441	920	292	872	730	2814	1660	4474	15.20
West Bengal	8875	27	4	37	29	97	483	580	6.54
Union Territories	1096	18	5	28	15	66	425	491	44.80
Total	328727	17497	8668	13325	10331	49820	35535	85355	25.97

Note: (i) For standard definitions of various categories of land use adopted in the land utilization statistics, refer to Annexure I.

Source: www.indiastat.com, State of Forest Report, 2001 and Statistical Abstract of Arunachal Pradesh, 2003.

of CPRs in Arunachal Pradesh is mainly because of large CPRF area.

(iii) The states where the CPRs fall under the category of 'medium' level of CPRs are Bihar (27.71), Goa (28.39), Gujarat (30.38), Madhya Pradesh (26.81), Orissa (33.95), Assam (33.96), Rajasthan (40.00), Sikkim (40.99) and Tripura (26.22). The Union Territories as a single unit come under this category with 44.80 per cent of CPRs. The extent of CPRs in Gujarat, Madhya Pradesh and Rajasthan is associated with the higher area under 'PPGL' and 'CWL'.

(iv) The states where CPRs is 'low' i.e., less than or around 25 per cent of geographical area are Andhra Pradesh (22.74), Maharashtra (20.74), Tamil Nadu (19.48), Karnataka (18.77), Uttar Pradesh (15.20), Punjab (7.78), West Bengal (6.54), Haryana (6.45), Kerala (3.60) and Jammu and Kashmir (2.54). Among these low CPRs category states, Punjab, West Bengal, Haryana, Kerala and Jammu and Kashmir are accounted very low CPRs to their total area. These states except Jammu and Kashmir have a high level of agricultural development and so a higher percentage of the land under private ownership with low level of per capita forest exists.

In terms of the per capita CPRs area, the states above the national average of 0.084 hectares per head per annum in 2001 are found in the North East Region, Orissa, Madhya Pradesh, Himachal Pradesh and Gujarat while the rest states are registered below the average.

So far we have discussed the regional variations of CPRs in India. The discussion will remain incomplete, if we do not analyse the degree of dependency on CPRs. In this regard, the 54th Round of NSSO Data (1999) reveals the degree of dependency on CPRs. As per the estimates of it, a majority of the households depend on CPR land and forest resources for their requirements of fuelwood, fodder, bamboo and fish followed by medicinal plants and herbs, leaf biomass and fruits. There are indications that these CPRs flows have come down over time. Between 1993 and 1998, the extent of consumption of fuelwood from CPR land and forest resources has come down significantly at the all India level from 87 per cent of households to 62 per cent. The extent to which fuelwood consumption from CPR land and forest, in case of Rajasthan declines from 94 per cent to 34 per cent and for Haryana from 90 per cent to 41 per cent. Only 45 per cent of rural households reported collecting firewood from the commons now. The quantity collected in 1998 was just half of the quantity of fuelwood actually consumed. In term of value of collections, around 40 percent of fish comes from the CPRs, 25 per cent from leaf biomass and around 16 per cent from fodder and bamboo. The details are given in Table 3.4.

STATUS OF PROPERTY RIGHTS AND CPRs IN ARUNACHAL PRADESH

In the present study area, the property rights structure rests with three regimes i.e., public property, private property, and community property. All land in a village, theoretically, was community land and the management which was under the village council or the village chief. The village chief (popularly known as *Gaon Burah*), as the leader of the village used to decide which plots were to be brought under shifting cultivation (locally known as *jhuming*), when agricultural operations would be undertaken, when and where would hunting or fishing be done (Das, 1995). In the matter of common interest like construction of village road, tracks and footpaths, bridge etc, the village head used to mobilize the communal labour in this regard. (Chowdhury, 1982). Thus, in the absence of separate economic institutions, economic activities are organized by the tribal socio-political organizations. A brief overview is given to draw an account of the ownership pattern on land and forests along with the natural process of evolution among the different tribal communities of Arunachal Pradesh based on some villages studied by the Agro Economic

Table 3.4: Average Value of Collections from CPRs and Average Consumption Expenditure across Different States of India

State	Percentage of Households Using Fuelwood		Percentage of Households Reporting Collection in 1998	Average Quantity (in kilogram)	
	1998	1993-94		Collected in 1998	Consumed in 1993-94
Andhra Pradesh	81	94	59	545	950
Arunachal Pradesh	85	96	82	5448	3787
Assam	60	97	44	614	141
Bihar*	58	70	41	446	623
Gujarat	73	83	55	483	877
Haryana	41	90	27	306	1013
Himachal Pradesh	59	91	56	1080	2346
Jammu & Kashmir	51	89	33	553	2234
Karnataka	79	96	53	484	1446
Kerala	53	95	13	204	1301
Madhya Pradesh*	76	96	56	621	1673
Maharashtra	67	82	59	522	776

Manipur	75	96	40	1157	1635
Meghalaya	93	94	86	2558	2282
Mizoram	98	99	97	6688	1532
Nagaland	98	99	67	2972	2816
Orissa	75	91	62	944	1290
Punjab	69	74	24	550	841
Rajasthan	34	94	21	267	1368
Sikkim	69	74	53	1805	1832
Tamil Nadu	70	93	61	497	816
Tripura	51	97	31	427	1417
Uttar Pradesh*	51	88	33	416	813
West Bengal	51	73	38	324	742
India	62	87	45	500	1015

Note: 1. Annual consumption expenditure is derived from the estimates taken from Sarvekshana, Vol. XXIV, Issue no.84 (July-September, 2000,p.74).

2. The symbol asterisk (*) are the states prior to the formation of new states.

Research Centre, Jorhat and the Law Research Institution, Guwahati.

The Adis of East Siang, Upper Siang and West Siang districts were predominantly *jhumias*. The terrain and mountainous landscape of the land where they settled is conducive for *jhum* cultivation. The system of *jhum* cultivation prevalent among different sub-tribes of the Adi-group has a system of individual ownership of cultivable *jhum* land. For example, the individual family returns to the first plot after each *jhum* cycle. This led to private property, not by formal but by informal convention among the group or the clan. However, the clan and community ownership was found in forest areas.

The Nyishis of Lower Subansiri, Papum Pare and East Kameng districts also practise *jhum* cultivation extensively. The system which they adopt in *jhum* is quite opposite to that of the Adi tribe groups. They usually do not return to the same plot after a *jhum* cycle. Thus lands not taken up by the individual members of the community remained as village common land where no one exercises the rights of ownership.

On the other hand, the Wanchos, the Noctes, the Khamptis of Changlang, Tirap and Lohit districts had evolved a hierarchical society under a well organized system of chieftainship. According to the system of chieftainship, all land surrounding the village belongs to the village common land. The village chief and the village council together used to allot this common village land to the individual members of the community. In case of abandonment of any land by anybody (e.g., migration to another area or dead etc), the land was automatically reverted to the village common land. Hence individual ownership was non-transferable but permanent by virtue of right of inheritance within the tribe. In case of forest and fishing areas, these communities treated it as village commons.

The Apatanis of Lower Subansiri and the Khamti of Lohit district are the only tribes who practiced permanent cultivation in Arunachal Pradesh. The Apatanis are famous for their skill-oriented agricultural farming. Individual ownership in cultivable land was full and complete in all respects. They were tribes which recognized the intra-tribe but inter-village mobility with equal footing in case of land ownership. The clan as well as community ownership was recognized in the forest areas falling under the village jurisdiction.

The Monpas developed extensive terrace cultivation along with *jhum* cultivation. Both individual as well as community ownership evolved in the Monpa society. Individual ownership is predominant in cultivable land while the village council (*Mangma*) controls mainly village forests and pastures. The village council can lease out its land to the individuals in exchange of some annual tax. The homestead land belongs to the village commons and the members of the community enjoy non-transferable permanent ownership rights over this property.

The majority of the sub-tribes of Mishmi of Lohit and Anjaw district also practised Adi type *jhum* cultivation. They inherit ownership and users' right over land through either the clan or the village council headed by the village elders and the *Gaon Burah*. They treat all land including homestead land as village commons. Buying and selling of such lands are possible within the Mishmi tribes but not possible or transferable among intra-tribes. Traditionally, the village lands were bartered for livestock or kinds. The *jhum* lands under the control of an individual always remain an inheritance property of the family and no member from the village or community has right to claim over the property. In case, if no one is left to inherit the property, it automatically converts to the village commons and the village council of the *Gaon Burah* looks after the property. This ownership system led to private property, not by formal but by informal convention among the group or the clan. However, the clan or the community ownership was strictly found in the rural areas. On the other hand, in the plains of Lohit district and under the semi-urban areas, lands are owned privately through informal conventions of occupancy and users' right.

It appears from the forgoing discussion that both the land-use and the agricultural practices had some bearing on the land ownership pattern. While some sort of individual ownership was found to be dominant factors in case of cultivable land, community and of clan ownership was the general form in the fishing and forest areas. In case of cultivable land, the degree of individual property right varies from tribe to tribe. Those tribes which practised Adi-type *jhum* cultivation in general, attained a kind of preliminary individual ownership. However, there are some tribes which practised Nyishi type *jhum* cultivation and in those cases even cultivable land belonged to the category of village land.

However, the property rights formations in Arunachal Pradesh have undergone substantial changes over the last many years. After Independence of the country, there was a gradual transformation from non-monetized to monetized economy. The process of monetization, commercialization, and subsequent differentiation led to the emergence of private property in land in a limited scale in some areas. Thus, in the post-Independence period the process continued with the active help of the state machinery. The land ownership pattern in contemporary Arunachal Pradesh is diverse and changing. The unevenness in the development process has increased this diversity as well.

The only legal framework concerning land ownership in Arunachal Pradesh is the Jhum Land Regulation, 1947 which only recognizes the ownership to a piece of *jhum* land. As we have found that most of the land in Arunachal Pradesh was owned by the communities and some of them have been privatized in the recent decades. However, in case of privately owned land, the right of use and occupancy as well as the right of inheritance are generally enjoyed by the members of respective communities but the right to transfer is not total and unconditional (Mishra, 2001).

4

Socio-economic Profile of the Study Area

The present study attempts to analyse the linkages between forest dependency and CPRs particularly, forest resources. Out of the sixteen districts of the State, two districts namely, Lohit and Anjaw districts are taken as a case study. In both the districts, nine villages (three villages from Anjaw district and six villages from Lohit district) were selected for the detailed empirical study. Therefore, it will be interesting to give a brief socio-economic profile of Arunachal Pradesh, in general and the selected districts as well as the surveyed villages, in particular. Hence, an attempt is made in this chapter to analyse the socio-economic profile of the State on the basis of selected indicators and then the selected districts as well as surveyed villages.

A BRIEF SOCIO-ECONOMIC PROFILE OF ARUNACHAL PRADESH

Arunachal Pradesh (earlier known as NEFA) has a territory of 83,734 square kilometre, which is about 2.55 per cent of India's land area and one-third area of the North East India (32.83 per cent excluding Sikkim). Being the largest State (in terms of area) in North East India, Arunachal's area is slightly more than that of Assam, but its population is 0.11 per cent of India's population and only 2.58 per cent of the population of North East India. The population density in Arunachal Pradesh is 13 people per square kilometre against the all India average of 324 people per square kilometre as per 2001 Census.

Arunachal Pradesh has around 96 per cent hill terrain and its elevations range from 100 metre on the edge of Assam to about 7,000 metre on its northern borders. Wide variation in altitude coupled with abundance of rainfall has given rise to wide variations in climatic conditions within the State. This, in turn, has endowed the region with rich biodiversity. The richness of biodiversity is almost matched by its ethnic diversity. For example, Arunachal Pradesh is the home to 26 major tribes and 110 sub-tribes and minor tribes. The details of different tribes that inhabit different districts of Arunachal Pradesh are given in Table 4.1.

Arunachal Pradesh experienced the launch of development programme only after Independence of the country. At the time of Independence, Arunachal Pradesh was basically a monoeconomy, which was based on subsistence agriculture and forests. As far as the infrastructural facilities are concerned, the State had three jeepable roads with a total length of around 170 kilometers, three primary schools with an enrolment of around 30 students and thirteen primary health centres (Techno-Economic Survey of NEFA, 1967). However, since Independence the situation has undergone a notable change with the gradual transformation of the economy from non-monetised to the market economy (Mitra, 2006). With this background, the North Eastern Frontier Agency (NEFA) in 1964 asked the National Council of Applied Economic Research (NCAER) to conduct a techno-economic survey of NEFA. The Council in its report published in 1967 recommended action in three areas on a priority basis: (i) transport access both to and within the territory, (ii) development of natural resources, and (iii) improvement of social infrastructure. Based on the recommendation, it is found that the highest priority had been accorded to the infrastructural development particularly in road constructions in almost all the five-year plans. The approach and strategy adopted under the various plans is reflected in the distribution of the plan outlay under different plan periods of the State as shown in Table 4.2.

Table 4.1: District-wise Main Tribes of Arunachal Pradesh

District	Headquarters	The Main Tribes that Inhibit the District
Tawang	Tawang	Monpa
West Kameng	Bomdila	Monpa, Sherdukpen, Lishpa, Chugppa, Aka, Miji
East Kameng	Seppa	Nyishi, Sulung
Papum Pare	Yupia	Nyishi
Lower Subansiri	Ziro	Apatani, Nyishi
Upper Subansiri	Daporijo	Adi, Tagin
West Siang	Along	Adi, Memba
East Siang	Pasighat	Adi, Mishing
Upper Siang	Yingkiong	Adi
Dibang Valley	Anini	Idu Mishmi
Lohit	Tezu	Mishmi, Khampti, Singpho
Changlang	Changlang	Tangsa, Singpho
Tirap	Khonsa	Nocte, Wangcho
Kurung Kumey	Koloriang	Nyishi, Sulung, Tagin
Lower Dibang Valley	Roing	Mishmi, Adi (Padam)
Anjaw	Hawai	Mishmi, Meyor (Zekhring)

Source: Arunachal Pradesh Human Development Report, 2005, p.5.

Table 4.2 shows that from the inception of the plan, the main priority has been accorded to the development of economic infrastructure viz., transport and communication sector. This is due to the centrally push-plan to accelerate the development process through the creation of infrastructural facilities and expansion of social services like education. However, the share of power and irrigation including energy showed an increasing trend from 6.87 per cent in the Fifth Five-year Plan to 20.93 per cent at the end of the Ninth Five-year Plan. However, in the Tenth Five-year Plan, it was reduced to 18.55 per cent.

Table 4.2: Sectoral Plan Outlay in Arunachal Pradesh since the Fifth Five-year Plan

(in per cent)

Sector	V Plan (1974-79)	VI Plan (1980-85)	VII Plan (1985-90)	VIII Plan (1992-97)	IX Plan (1997-2002)	X Plan (2002-07)
Agriculture & Allied Services	26.77	20	21.66	20.24	13.16	18.11
Industry & Mining	2.05	2.1	2.41	1.91	1.29	1.78
Power & Irrigation	6.87	17.9	15.92	19.59	20.93	18.55
Transport & Communication	33.03	31.6	32.19	28.12	26.04	25.1
Community Services	30.84	27.6	26.62	26.08	33.03	29.83
Economic Services	0.44	0.4	0.66	1.92	3.26	4.64
General Services	0	0.4	0.54	2.14	2.29	1.99
Total	100	100	100	100	100	100

Note: Although in 1953, the State was in the First Five-year Plan, but the planning process in Arunachal Pradesh was intensified only since the Fifth Five Plan onwards.

Source: 1. Basic Statistics of North Eastern Region, 2002.
2. Government of Arunachal Pradesh Draft Tenth Five-year Plan, Department of Planning, Government of Arunachal Pradesh, Itanagar (*www.arunachalpradesh.nic.in*).

Selecting the growth of per capita Net State Domestic Product (NSDP) as a measure of economic performance, it was found that the per capita NSDP experienced an exponential average growth rate of 4.03 per cent in the 1970's and 4.69 per cent in the 1980's against the all India average of 1.10 per cent and 2.85 per cent respectively during the same periods. The high growth rate of income is due to the grants-in-aid of the centre, which constitute nearly 60 per cent of its NSDP. Table 4.3 shows a brief comparison between the exponential growth rate of Net National Product (NNP) and NSDP of Arunachal Pradesh.

Table 4.3: Growth Rate of NNP and NSDP

(in per cent)

Period	Growth rate of		Growth rate of Per capita	
	NNP	NSDP	NNP	NSDP
1971-80	3.36	7.07	1.1	4.03
1981-90	4.99	7.81	2.85	4.69
1991-2000	5.93	4.81	3.95	2.31

Note: NNP data are from Economic Survey, 2003-04, Government of India and NSDP data are from State Domestic Product of Arunachal Pradesh for different years published by the Directorate of Economics and Statistics, Government of Arunachal Pradesh, Itanagar.

Table 4.3 demonstrates that the economy of Arunachal Pradesh grew rapidly in both 1970's and 1980's but lost some of its initial momentum in the 1990's. A comparison of the growth of the State with the national economy presents a mixed dimension. For example, the growth of NSDP was markedly higher than the growth of NNP in the 1970's as well as in the 1980's. However, in the 1990's, the national economy performed better than the State economy. The policy of economic reforms pursued by the centre in the 1990's seems to have released forces propelling the national economy to a higher growth path, but in the same decade, the Arunachal Pradesh economy slid to a lower growth path.

However, the infrastructure facilities are inadequate even now and the State is lagging behind the national and regional average in most of components of infrastructure. At the same time Arunachal Pradesh has still one of the poorest health conditions in the country. Its life expectancy of 54.05 years in 2000 is the lowest among the fifteen major states whose life tables are available (Human Development Report of Arunachal Pradesh, 2005). There were five districts of Arunachal Pradesh whose life expectancy at birth was below 50 years.

Thus, with the persistently high income growth, Arunachal Pradesh economy has undergone some structural transformation. The relative importance of agriculture in NSDP has declined. This relative decline of agriculture has, however, not been accompanied with the relative expansion of the secondary sector but with the rapid expansion of the tertiary sector. Even within the secondary sector, the contribution of the manufacturing sector was accounting for around 4 per cent of the State income. The details are shown in the Table 4.4.

Table 4.4: Sectoral Contribution to NSDP of Arunachal Pradesh

(in per cent)

Period	Sector			
	Primary	Secondary	Tertiary	Total
1970-71	59.19	20.33	20.48	100
1980-81	47.28	32.21	20.51	100
1990-91	46.19	21.56	32.25	100
2001-02	36.88	22.16	40.96	100

Source: Based on Estimates of State Domestic Product, Directorate of Economics and Statistics, Government of Arunachal Pradesh, Itanagar, 2002.

The agriculture of the State has undergone some substantial changes over the last thirty years. Shifting cultivation also known as 'slash-and-burn agriculture' or 'rotational bush fallow agriculture' and as '*jhum* cultivation' or '*jhuming*' in North East India, which is an ancient method of agricultural farming, has relatively declined in recent years, giving a way to permanent cultivation, which is now the generator of the major portion of agricultural income in the State. However, the continuance of *jhuming* in the State is closely linked to ecological, socio-economic, and cultural and absence of property rights among tribal communities. Since the communities in general own the land, the *Village Council* or *Gaon Burah* or village elders divide the *jhum* land among families for their subsistence on it. At the same time, the government has given much emphasis for the development of agro-forestry, sericulture and horticulture as alternatives or supplementary activities on the hill slopes of the State.

On the other hand, Arunachal Pradesh has made a very significant progress in literacy. With only a 7.12 per cent literacy rate in 1961, the State covered a long route in the course of four decades in achieving a 54.74 per cent literacy rate by 2001 Census. Hence, the average growth of literacy stood at 1.09 per cent per annum and in the process, it has overtaken some States like Bihar and Rajasthan etc.

From the above analysis, it is found that the State has achieved a significant development in transport and communication, agriculture, income and literacy. As far as the Human Development Index (HDI) is concerned, it shows a precarious situation of the State. According to the Human Development Report, 2005, the HDI for Arunachal Pradesh is estimated to be 0.515 for the year 2001 which is one of the lowest among fifteen major States of India. Thus the backwardness of the State as compared to the national average may be due to many factors like its late start in the development process, the long isolation from the market, geographical remoteness etc.

As far as the forest land is concerned, almost all the tribes of the State have the community forest which is under the exclusive control of the village council. In some cases, clan ownership is also recognized in the forest areas falling within the village jurisdiction. The unclassified State Forest i.e., the area under community forest, on the basis of legal status of forests in the State, was found to be 38.57 per cent of the total area or 61.43 per cent of the recorded forest area of the State. However, the emergence of individual forest ownership has been observed in the State as a whole. It is of recent phenomenon in the constitutional shift from community forest ownership to individual forest ownership in the ownership pattern of forests. The detailed classification of forests in Arunachal Pradesh is shown in Table 4.5.

Table 4.5: Classification of Forests in Arunachal Pradesh in 2001

Legal Status of Forests	Area in '000 hectares	Percentage of State area	Percentage of Reported Forest area
Reserved Forests	1988	23.74	38.57
Protected Forests*	0.78	0.01	0.02
Unclassified State Forests	3166	37.36	61.43

Note: Protected Forest data is compiled from *Statistical Abstract*, 2004
Source: State of Forest Report, 2001, FSI, MoEF, GOI

The reserve forests constituted 38.57 per cent which is less than the all India average of 53.09 per cent. However, there has been a steady compound growth of 7 hectare per annum in reserve forest as compared to 1950 where only 53 thousand hectare was under the reserve forests in the State.

BACKGROUND OF LOHIT AND ANJAW DISTRICTS

Let us have an overview on the socio-economic profile of the study area i.e., Lohit and Anjaw districts. There were a number of administrative changes before coming into existence of the present Lohit and Anjaw districts. The present Lohit district has inter-district borders with Anjaw district on the North-East, Lower Dibang Valley district on the North-West and Changlang district on the South and inter-state boarder with Assam on the West (Fig. 4.1).

Fig. 4.1: Administrative Map of Lohit District, Arunanchal Pradesh

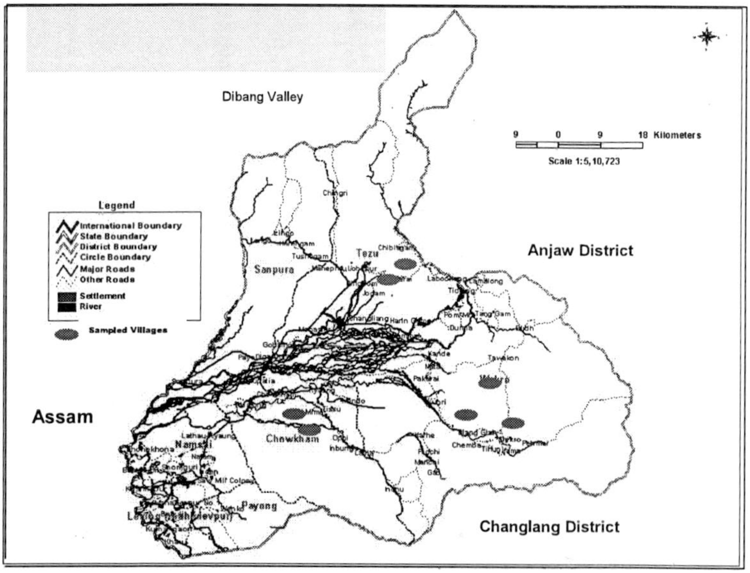

Source: Arunachal Pradesh Remote Sensing and Application Centre, Itanagar

On the other hand, Anjaw district has international borders with China on the East and the North and Myanmar on the South-East. It has inter district boarders with Lohit district on the West and Upper Dibang Valley on the North West (Map:4.2).

In 1914, the North East Frontier Tract was constituted with three administrative units: the Central and Eastern Sections, the Lakhimpur Frontier Tract and the Western Section and the area covered by these districts became a part of the Central and Eastern Sections. In 1919, the Central and Eastern Sections were renamed as the Sadia Frontier Tract. In 1943, a new administrative charge was created with inclusion of certain area from the Sadia Frontier Tract and the Lakhimpur Frontier Tract and was named as the Tirap Frontier Tract. Under the North-East Frontier Tracts (Internal Administrative) Regulation, 1948, the remaining portion of Sadia

Fig. 4.2: Administrative Map of Anjaw District, Arunanchal Pradesh

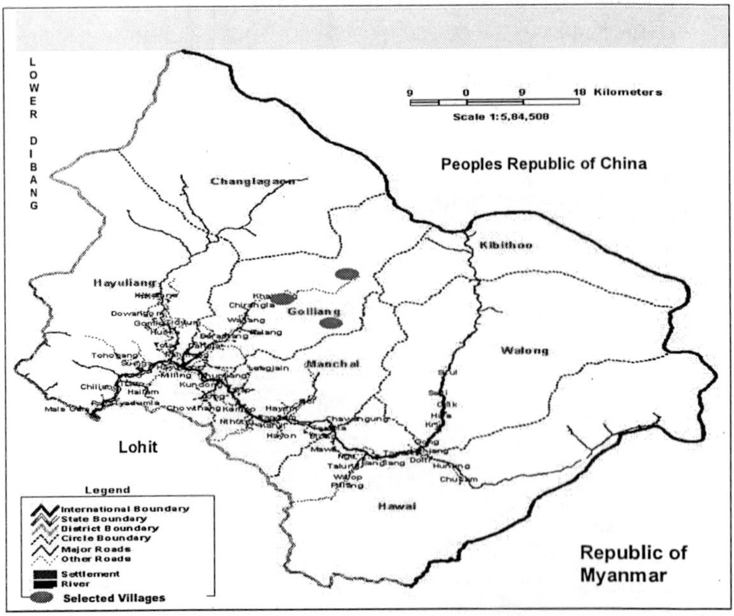

Source: Arunachal Pradesh Remote Sensing and Application Centre, Itanagar

Frontier Tract was divided into two administrative units as the Abor Hills district and the Mishmi Hills district with their headquarters at Pasighat and Sadia. In 1951, the plains of the Mishmi Hills district were transferred to Assam. In 1952, the headquarter of the Mishmi Hills district was shifted to Tezu. In 1954, as the administrative nomenclature of the territory was changed from the North East Frontier Tract to the North East Frontier Agency, the Mishmi Hills district was renamed as the Lohit Frontier Division. In 1965, under the North-East Frontier Agency (Administrative) Regulation, 1965, the Lohit Frontier Division came to be known as Lohit district. After Arunachal Pradesh became the Union Territory, a number of administrative changes took place and as a result, Lohit district was divided into two districts namely Lohit district and Dibang Valley district in June 1980 under the Arunachal Pradesh (Re-organisation of

District) Act 1980. Further, Lohit district was bifurcated into two districts namely Lohit district and Anjaw district with their headquarters at Tezu and Hawai in February 2004 under the Arunachal Pradesh Re-organisation of Districts Amendment Bill though it was deemed to have come into force in December 2003. Thus, Anjaw district became the youngest and the sixteenth district of the State.

The tribes like the *Taraons* or *Tawarahs* or *Digaru Mishmis* which is a sub-tribe of the Mishmis, the Idu Mishmis, the Khamptis and the Singphos inhabit Lohit district while the Mishmis sub-tribe *Kamans* or *Miju Mishmis* and the Zekhrings (*Meyor*) tribe are the major group of people who dwell in Anjaw district. The Mishmis follow animistic way of life and worship different deities, and many more living and non-living objects like sun, moon, sky, rocks, mountains, forests, river streams, earth, fire etc which they believe of having Supernatural beings both benevolent and malevolent power in nature. They have very strong cultural practices of offering efficacious things like egg, fowl, spirituous liquor, pig, cattle, Mithun (*Bos frontalis*), cloth, pieces of leads etc., in case of sickness, ill luck and variety of calamities for which they are sometimes called as devil worshippers. There are also other ritual ceremonies, prayers taboos, incantations performed by the Mishmi tribes to have religious moral and philosophical wish to prolong life, to ward off evil, to obtain children and to destroy or harass sworn enemies. In Taraon dialect, the Supreme creator is addressed as *Jabmalu* and in Kaman dialect, it is addressed as *Matai*. They believe that all the present form of life and power to heal and to protect their life is bestowed by the Creator. The Sun God is known as either *Ringya* (in Taraon dilect) or *Amik* (in Kaman dialect) and is regarded as the '*God of Truth and Justice*'. The Mishmis swear by *Him* if it is invoked for attesting or seeking truth. They follow patriarchy and practice both shifting and permanent types of cultivation. They rear Mithun (*Bos frontalis*), cattle, buffaloes, pony, pigs and fowls. They do hunting with guns, bow and arrows, net angle and trap.

The Khamties and the Singphoes are religious and pious tribe, and they are known for their hospitality. The Khamties inhibit in and around Tengapani basin of Namsai Circle in Lohit district. Both the Khamties and the Singphoes follow Hinayana sect of Buddhism. The Khamties have their own language which is known as *Tai Khampti*.

The Zekhrings live in the hilly terrain and banks of the Lohit River in Walong and Kibithoo area of Anjaw district. They follow the Mahayana sect of Buddhism blended with traditional animist beliefs. They are ethically and linguistically related to the Kamans and the Tibetans.

It was observed that all the indigenous tribes of these districts are pluralistic society which represents a picture of transparent homogeneity and heterogeneity within multi-racial, multi-religious and multi-lingual bases of culture. Regarding the demography, a contrast between Anjaw district and Lohit district in terms to economic development is quite apparent. It shows economic backwardness and lack of even basic social and economic facilities in higher altitude, basically mountains and its surroundings whereas it is comparatively better in the foothills and plains.

The present Lohit district covers a geographical area of 5,212 square kilometre (6.22 per cent of the total geographical area of the State) spread over to 206 villages and two Census towns. It has a population of 1,25,086 people (which is 11.39 per cent of the State population) as per the 2001 Census. On the other hand, Anjaw district covers an area of 6,190 square kilometre (7.39 per cent of the State area) with 281 villages but no Census towns. The population of the district in 2001 Census is 18,441 people (which is around 1.68 per cent of the State population). The population density of Lohit and Anjaw districts are recorded at twenty four and three people per square kilometre respectively while the literacy rate of Lohit district is 62.42 per cent and Anjaw district 19.2 per cent as against the State average of 54.74 per cent. Porter tracks and mule paths were the main road communication that existed in the area of Lohit district during the pre-Independence and early 1950's. With the initiative of the State government, the length of roads (both surfaced and unsurfaced) constructed so far in Lohit district (including Anjaw district) is around 806 kilometre only during 2002-03 and the road density of both the districts is 9.63 per cent per 100 square kilometre. The number of villages having road connectivity was 40.70 per cent as on 1997.

In health infrastructure, the present Lohit district has one district hospital, three community health centres, four primary health centres and twelve sub-centres with two homeopathy centres. On the other hand, Anjaw district has only two community health centres, three primary health centres, thirteen sub-centres with one homeopathy centre. The total number of beds installed in all health centres in Lohit district stood at 199 beds during 2003-04. The lone district hospital has a capacity of ninety four beds only. On the other hand, there is no district hospital till today in Anjaw district but it has a community health centre with a capacity of thirty beds at Hayuliang, the administrative sub-division of the district. The total number of beds available during 2003-04 in Anjaw district stood at fifty eight beds. The total numbers of doctors available in these two districts are forty one doctors and thereby serving around 3500 people per doctor. Thus, the health services are a matter of concern and need concerted efforts from both Government and Non-Governmental Organisations in both the districts. Out of the nine surveyed villages, only three villages, namely, Loiliang, Danglat and Soolungtoo villages in Lohit district have primary health centres within the village. However, in other surveyed villages, there is no primary health centre. They reported that in earlier days people suffered from all types of diseases like, malaria, cholera, chicken pox, diarrhea, dysentery etc. It took a heavy toll of human life in the villages as no proper medical facilities or vaccines were easily available. It is also reported that herbal medicine like *Mishmi Tita* and Poppy (which is locally known as *Kani*) are used as an alternative medicine for all types of pain, ache, diseases etc. in consultation with elders or traditional healers. They believe that a sick person should not be taken directly to hospital as long as they are traditionally or customarily confirmed for the presence of ghost spirit or supernatural power from the pulse count or rituals sacrificing either a fowl or a pig or a *mithun* depending on the seriousness of the disease. They are the people who refrain from visiting hospitals or doctors as much as possible, mostly due to superstitious belief, economic problems and less awareness of the modern medical facilities. The distance to health centres and transportation problem along with unavailability of doctors and medicines and absence of private doctors hinder them for visiting hospitals and doctors. In very serious cases, they do visit the Assam Medical College, Dibrugarh or the Ram Krishna Mission Hospital, Itanagar. The situation is changing slowly. Most of the literate people are becoming aware of modern medicine and available health facilities.

PROFILE OF THE SURVEYED VILLAGES

In this sub-section, an attempt is made to provide a brief profile of the villages surveyed. The villages selected for the study are Kasanglat, Kaniliang, Brailiang, Loiliang, Danglat, Solungtoo, Chireng, Karhe and Tillang Kyong. Out of these villages, the first three villages are inhabited by the *Kamans* or *Miju Mishmis* and are located in Anjaw district under Goiliang Circle of the administrative unit of Hayuliang sub-division and the remaining six villages are located in Lohit district. Out of the six villages of Lohit district, the first two villages are inhabited mainly by both the *Taraons* or *Tawarahs* or *Digaru Mishmis* and the *Kamans* and are located under Tezu Circle of the administrative unit of Tezu sub-division. Chireng, Karhe and Tillang Kyong are inhabited by the *Kamans* or *Miju Mishmis* and are located under Wakro Circle of the administrative unit of Namsai sub-division while the last village, Solungtoo is inhabited by the Khampti tribe and is under Namsai Circle of the administrative unit of Namsai sub-division. Regarding the altitude, all the three villages under Hayuliang sub-division are found at the range of around 1000-1500 metre. The villages under Tezu sub-division are located at 200-250 metre while the villages under Namsai sub-division like, Chireng, Karhe, and Tillang Kyong villages are located at around 700 metre and Solungtoo at around 140 metre above the sea level. (The details are given in Table 1.1).

Table 4.6: Socio-economic Characteristics of the Surveyed Villages

Name of Village	Average Size of Households	Average Years of Schooling	Average Size of Operational Holdings (in ha)	Average Value of Livestock Reared (in '000 rupee)
Kasanglat	4.93	2.89	5.16	10.21
Kaniliang	4.17	0.95	4.31	7.49
Brailiang	5.53	1.26	3.28	8.9
Loiliang	4.08	4.32	4.04	6.39
Danglat	3.6	2.33	3.96	10.66
Soolungtoo	5.98	2.64	5.85	13.46
Chireng	6.08	2	5.06	7.4
Karhe	7.63	1,23	4.69	12.62
Tillang Kyong	8.38	1.16	4.73	12.76

Source: Survey Data, 2005-06.

Kasanglat village is situated in the steep mountainous slope and eastern bank of Dav River while Kaniliang and Brailiang villages are situated in the upper flat slopes on the southern bank of Brai River, which are tributaries of the Lohit River. On the other hand, Loiliang is situated in plain lands near the foothills. Danglat and Sotungtoo villages are situated in plain lands while Chireng village is situated on the foothills and Karhe village on the lower slope of the Patkai mountain. However, Tillang Kyong is situated in a picturesque landscape vale surrounded by the lower ridges of the Patkai mountain from all directions. The villagers, in Anjaw district, mainly practice jhum cultivation while the villages, in Lohit district practice both permanent as well as jhum cultivation. Agriculture is the main source of livelihood of the people of surveyed villages. Taking all the sample households together, we find that the average size of holdings is around 4.54 hectare. However, there are variations among the villages surveyed. The details are shown in Table 4.6.

If we undertake an analysis of other social infrastructural facilities like, connectivity, health, education etc. available to these villages, it is found that there is a high variation among these indicators. The details of such infrastructural facilities of the surveyed villages are given in Table 4.7.

Table 4.7 shows that around 33 per cent of the surveyed villages have jeepable road facility. Out of these villages, Loiliang, Soolungtoo and Danglat villages in Lohit district have better health, education and connectivity facilities than any other village. As these villages are in plain areas and nearer to the district headquarter, these villages have better accessibility. However, the average distance from villages to the jeepable road in the study area is found to be 6.11 kilometre. The average distance from the surveyed villages to the nearest bus stop is around 14 kilometre. All the surveyed villages do not have higher secondary school, but Loiliang and Soolungtoo villages are the surveyed villages which have a secondary school. None of the surveyed villages in Anjaw district has either a primary or middle school. For sending the children to primary school, the villagers have to come down at Goiliang and for middle school it is at Hayuliang, the administrative sub-division of Anjaw district. Among the surveyed villages in Lohit district, Loiliang, Soolungtoo and Danglat villages have both primary and middle schools in their villages. However, Solungtoo, Karhe and Tillang Kyong villages have only primary school.

The health services in rural areas are provided through community health sub-centres, primary health centres, hospitals etc. There are only two surveyed villages which have the primary health centres. In some surveyed villages like Kasanglat,

Table 4.7: Infrastructural Facilities in the Surveyed Villages

(Distance in kilometre)

Name of Village	Jeepable Road	Bus Stop	Post Office	Market	Primary Health Centre	Pre/ Primary School	Middle School	Secondary School	Higher Secondary School
Kasanglat	4	20	20	20	6	6	20	20	20
Kaniliang	8	25	25	25	5	5	25	25	25
Brailiang	10	30	30	30	7	7	30	30	30
Loiliang	0	0	12	12	0	0	0	0	12
Danglat	0	0	8	8	0	0	0	8	8
Solungtoo	0	0	10	10	0	0	0	0	10
Chireng	2	2	2	2	2	2	2	2	59
Karhe	5	9	9	9	9	0	9	9	75
Tillang Kyong	26	39	39	39	39	0	39	39	99

Source: Survey Data, 2005-06.

Kaniliang, Brailiang, Soolungtoo, Karhe and Tillang Kyong, the users have to walk more than 5 kilometre for availing themselves of the medical services from primary health centres.

A descriptive statistics of infrastructural facilities of villages surveyed is given in Table 4.8.

Table 4.8: Descriptive Statistics of Infrastructural Facilities in the Surveyed Villages

Distance from	Max.	Min.	Mean (in km.)	Standard Deviation (in km.)	Coefficient of Variation (in per cent)
Jeepable Road	26	0	6.11	8.28	73.78
Bus Stop	39	0	13.89	14.98	92.72
Post Office	39	2	17.22	12.09	142.44
Primary Health Centre	39	0	7.56	12.26	61.63
Primary School	7	0	2.22	2.95	75.37
Middle School	39	0	13.89	14.98	92.72
Secondary School	39	0	14.78	14.27	103.54
Higher Secondary School	99	8	37.56	32.49	115.58

Source: Survey Data, 2005-06.

Table 4.8 shows that the distance from post office of the surveyed villages is found to have a high degree of variation followed by the distance from higher secondary school, secondary school, middle school, bus stop, primary school, jeepable road and primary health centre respectively.

As far as ownership of natural resources are concerned, we find that there are growing emergence of private property rights in land. The details are given in Table 4.9.

Depending on the variation in social infrastructure, the ownership rights to land and to forest differ from one district to another. As far as land ownership is concerned, community owned land is found in Anjaw district while both private and community ownership to land prevail in Lohit district. However, the right to use and the right to transfer of land, in principle, are solely based on the occupancy as well as the right to inheritance among these tribes. In the context of Mishmi society, the youngest son inherits the lion's share of his father's property. He is also responsible to repay all the debts of his father. Daughters have no role in the inheritance even in absence of male child in the family. In such instances, the clan members or *Village Council* will inherit all the properties as well as the right to look after the daughters until they all are matured. However, at the time of marriage of the daughter, land is sometimes used as a gift to the groom family. Presently, rules are slowly changing due to the modernisation process as well as the shift from non-monetised economy to monetised economy. In some exceptional case of land transfer, an interesting case was observed during the field study trip that a piece of land was under the occupancy of a Nepalese woman who happened to be settled in the 1950's at Tezu town. When she wanted to return to her native village, she sold the land in cash to *a Kamans* through mutual understandings and negotiations but could not sell it to non-locals. Similar cases are also observed of selling land by non-locals to other tribes of Arunachal Pradesh particularly in urban areas. However, such cases are not yet reported to any legal agencies. The right to sale or transfer of land is generally allowed within the community itself, but inter-tribe selling or buying is yet to be found in these surveyed districts.

Forests are an indispensable part in the socio-economic and religious activities of these indigenous communities. It is, in general, owned collectively by them and they heavily depend on it for their survival. However, the emergence of private ownership of forests is recent phenomenon due to the introduction of monetised market economy and it is found in the villages of Danglat, Soolungtoo and Tillang Kyong of Lohit district. But, in all the villages of Anjaw district and Loiliang, Chireng and Karhe villages of Lohit district, forest ownership is bestowed by tradition to the community or Village Council which is called by the *Taraons* or *Tawarahs* as *Kebeya* or *Pharari* by the *Kamans*.

Table 4.9: Institutional Arrangements in the Surveyed Villages

Name of Village / Resource ownership	Kasanglat	Kaniliang	Brailiang	Loiliang	Danglat	Solungtoo	Chireng	Karhe	Tillang Kyong
1. Forest Land									
(a) Owned Collectively	3	3	3	3	×	×	3	3	×
(b) Owned Collectively with private ownership of village	×	×	×	×	3	3	×	×	3
(c) User rights to all members of village	3	3	3	3	×	×	3	3	×
(d) Open Access	3	3	3	×	×	×	×	×	×
(e) Use rights to villagers but others pay entry fee	×	×	×	×	×	3	×	×	×
(f) User rights to other villages of the same community	3	3	3	×	×	×	×	×	×
2. Cultivated Land									
(a) Owned Collectively	3	3	3	×	×	×	3	3	×
(b) Owned Collectively with private ownership of village	×	×	×	3	3	3	3	3	3

(c) User rights to all members of village	3	3	3	3	×	3	×	×	×
(d) Open Access	×	×	×	×	×	×	×	×	×
(e) Use rights to villagers but others pay entry fee	×	×	×	3	3	3	×	3	3
(f) User rights to other villages of the Same Community	×	×	×	×	×	3	×	×	×
3. Village Commons other than Forest									
(a) Owned Collectively	3	3	3	3	3	3	3	3	3
(b) Owned Collectively with private ownership of village	×	×	×	×	×	×	×	×	×
(c) User rights to all members of village	3	3	3	3	3	3	3	3	3
(d) Open Access	3	3	3	×	×	×	3	3	×
(e) Use rights to villagers but others pay entry fee	3	3	3	3	3	3	3	3	3
(f) User rights to other villages of the Same Community	3	3	3	×	×	×	3	3	3

Note: The tick (3) mark indicates the presence of attributes scale.
Source: Survey Data, 2005-06.

In other words, the ownership right to village commons other than forests rests mainly with community in Lohit district and both the village commons as well as the forests rest with community in Anjaw district.

Regarding the quality of forests, it also differs from one administrative sub-division to other sub-division in these districts. The quality of forests in the surveyed villages is shown in Table 4.10.

Table 4.10 indicates that the four villages viz., Kasanglat, Kaniliang, Brailiang and Tillang Kyong have dense forests while the remaining villages have degraded forests within 2 kilometers from the villages. On the other hand, within 5 kilometers from the village, Loiliang is the only village which have a moderately dense forests and Danglat and Solungtoo villages have degraded forests. However, Kasanglat, Kaniliang, Brailiang Chireng, Karhe and Tillang Kyong villages have dense forests within this limit. But, within 10 kilometers from the villages, all the villages except Soolungtoo and Danglat have dense forests. Trees are mainly used for fuelwood, fencing as well as construction of houses in all the surveyed villages of Anjaw district and Loiliang, Danglat and Soolungtoo in Lohit district. However, in Chireng, Karhe and Tillang Kyong villages under Wakro Circle of Namsai sub-division, Lohit district, bamboos are mainly used for these purposes as it is abundantly available in the vicinity of the villages. A general perception amongst the villagers about the forests cover was that 10 to 20 years back there was dense forests surrounding the villages. They are of the opinion that illegal felling of trees for commercial purpose as well as high dependency on forests products for household consumption such as firewood, house construction materials, fencing etc. are the main factors for the degradation of forests. In all the three villages of Anjaw district, they reported that they still collect firewood and other household materials within 2 kilometers. In the villages of Lohit district, villagers are now collecting these items within 5 to 10 kilometre distance from the surveyed villages except Chireng, Karhe and Tillang Kyong.

Table 4.10: Quality of Forests in the Surveyed Villages

Name of Village	Within 2 kms. from the Village			Within 5 kms. from the Village			Within 10 kms. from the Village		
	Dense	Moderate	Degraded	Dense	Moderate	Degraded	Dense	Moderate	Degraded
Kasanglat	3			3			3		
Kaniliang	3			3			3		
Brailiang	3			3			3		
Loiliang			3		3		3		
Danglat			3			3		3	
Solungtoo			3			3		3	
Chireng			3	3			3		
Karhe			3	3			3		
Tillang Kyong	3			3			3		

Note: The tick (3) mark indicates presence of the attributed scale.
Source: Survey Data, 2005-06.

5

Forest Dependency and Socio-economic Heterogeneity: An Econometric Analysis

In a transformation phase of the structure of political economy particularly, during the transitions from collective property rights regime to private property rights regime, the priorities and diverse realities of rural communities have often been largely misunderstood by institutions on community-based natural resource management (Wells and Brandon, 1992). These rural communities are far from homogeneity but rather heterogeneous in all walks of life. In fact, the relationship between socio-economic heterogeneity and distributional implications of community-based natural resource management is growing concern in participatory CPR management.

In need of social and institutional arrangements, the role of heterogeneity in commons management has tended to diverge in two schools of thought. The first pioneered by Olson (1965), and subsequently formalized in the theory of public goods, holds that inequality favours collective action. The second school of thought, which is closely associated with field study literature, insists that heterogeneity hampers collective action. For example, "Olson effects" demonstrated that considerable degree of inequality may favour provision of collective goods and suggested that inequality is beneficial to successful commons management. Bardhan and Dayton-Johnson (2000) in their case studies found that economic and social heterogeneity is consistently and significantly associated with lower levels of infrastructure management and a U-shaped relationship between inequality and commons management. Broadly, the taxonomy of socio-economic heterogeneity on which different scholars referred to the commons management are different types of heterogeneity like economic heterogeneity, cultural heterogeneity, ethnic heterogeneity and location heterogeneity etc. Economic heterogeneity which fundamentally refers to asymmetric distribution of wealth or income among the members of the resource-using groups; inequalities in the sacrifices of the community members make in cooperating with commons management; inequalities in the benefits they derived from such resources; and inequalities in outside earning opportunities is likely closely correlated with other form of heterogeneity. Despite the differences in the interpretation of relevant types of heterogeneity there is a consensus that heterogeneity is a factor in community-based resource management but there is no clear answer as to how and to what extent heterogeneity explains the dependency on CPRs. In this chapter, an attempt is made to explain in the context of Arunachal Pradesh where majority of the people in rural areas depend on community forests.

DETERMINANTS OF CONSUMPTION EXPENDITURE FROM COMMONS: AN ECONOMETRIC ANALYSIS

In order to explain the diverse intricacies of the dependency of rural community on community forests, an econometric model was developed to understand the relationship between forest dependency and socio-economic determinants. (Yanggen and Reardon, 2001 also adopted the same procedures). The extent of forest dependency is measured on the basis of the CPR based collections like timber, firewood, bamboo, leaf litter, herbs and medicinal plants, vegetables, eatable roots and wild animals hunted for consumption as part of total consumption expenditure by rural households as it was done in 54th round of NSS data (1999). It was hypothesized that household level benefits from common property forest resources (CPRF) would be associated with the household and community attributes. Hence, variation in forest dependency among rural households can be explained by the socio-economic status of user household. This relationship can be represented as:

$$\sum_{i}^{N} Y_{ji} = f\,(COSEX_i,\ HSIZE_i,\ LANDHO_i,\ GEN_i,\ EDU_i,\ LIVECOST_i,\ VIDMKT_i,\ CONNECTY_i)$$

Where,

Y	= Household consumption value derived from commons, (a proxy for household income from community forest in '000 rupce).
COSEX	= Total consumption expenditure of household (a proxy for income status of household in '000 rupee)
HSIZE	= Size of household i.e., number of family members in a household
LANDHO	= Size of land holdings in hectare
GEN	= Gender i.e., male = 1, female = 0
EDU	= Average education of family members (number of school year)
LIVECOST	= Value of livestock owned by household in '000 rupee
VIDMKT	= Average distance between house and market (a dummy variable for a house 17 km. and above =1 and below 17 km.= 0)
CONNECTY[1]	= Road connectivity between village and a constructed road (metal or non-metal) in km

1. Where the villages falling within a radius of one kilometre in hill terrain and 5 kilometre in the plains from a constructed road (pucca or kutcha) are considered as being connected as estimated by the Arunachal Public Works Department (1997).

'j' = Forest products (timber, firewood, bamboo, leaf litter, herbs and medicinal plants, vegetables, roots and wild animals etc.) and,

'i' = (1, 2, 3, . . ., N) observations.

Taking log in both sides, the standard equation is given as:

$$In \sum_{i=1}^{N} Y_{ji} = \beta_0 + \beta_1 InCOSEX_i + \beta_2 InHSIZE_i + \beta_3 InLANDHO_i$$
$$+ \beta_4 InGEN_i + \beta_5 InEDU_i + \beta_6 InLIVECOST_i + \beta_7 InVIDMKT_i$$
$$+ \beta_8 InCONNECTY_i + \varepsilon_i \quad (1)$$

The corresponding equation is defined as double-log model and it is based on a similar model by Di Falco and Perrings (2003) used to understand the effect of cooperative production on inter-specific crop genetic diversity.

It would have been better if the household level income from community forests is taken as a dependent variable. However, the estimation of income in Arunachal economy is, on the one hand, very difficult since the production at the village level is meant mainly for home consumption. On the other hand, the level of monetization is very low. Even after intensive survey, the income data suffers from a lot of errors. This is because the respondents normally hesitate in reporting his/her income. The level of literacy is very low in the study area. It is not possible to get the reliable income data at the household level. Hence, we have no other alternative but to take a proxy variable of household level consumption value from the community forest as well as total consumption expenditure of household. For consumption purpose again various edibles, fuel, house building materials etc. gathered from the CPRs are not generally marketed and their valuation is a problem. We have taken their imputed value in estimation of consumption. The data on quantities of different items gathered from forests are dependable but the problem is the non-existence of their village level prices. Some of these forest products are, no doubt, locally bartered but the exchange rate in barter does not reveal the absolute prices which are necessary to arrive at the value. Under these circumstances, we have to take into account of the prices of these products prevailing in the nearest local market.

The results of regression for determinants of household consumption value (Y) derived from commons on the above explanatory variables in the estimated equation is represented as:

$$
\begin{aligned}
In\widehat{Y}_{ji} = {} & \underset{(5.992)}{11.646^{*}} + \underset{(6.624)}{0.190^{*}}\, InCOSEX_i + \underset{(0.969)}{0.165}\, InHSIZE_i \\
& + \underset{(2.173)}{0.490^{**}}\, InLANDHO_i \\
& + \underset{(1.120)}{1.927}\, InGEN_i - \underset{(-\ 4.295)}{0.825^{*}}\, InEDU_i + \underset{(0.992)}{0.043}\, InLIVECOST_i \\
& + \underset{(9.447)}{16.413^{*}}\, InVIDMKT_i - \underset{(-\ 4.139)}{0.458^{*}}\, InCONNECTY_i
\end{aligned}
\qquad (2)
$$

$$R^2 = 0.54 \quad \overline{R}^2 = 0.53 \quad F = 44.356 \quad N = 312$$

Note: 1. The figures in parentheses are t-values

2. The asterisk symbol (* and **) denote significant at 0.01 and 0.05 level.

It is evident from the analysis that in addition to constant term, most of the estimators of explanatory variables are significant with the expected sign such as 'COSEX', 'EDU', 'VIDMKT' and 'CONNECTY' at 0.01 level and 'LANDHO' at 0.05 level (2-tailed). The R-square and adjusted R-square($\overline{R}^2$) for the estimation is as high as 54 per cent and 53 per cent respectively. The F-statistics for overall goodness of fit of the model is 44.36 which is highly significant at .00 = 0.000. The parameters of the log transformation variables like $\square_1$, $\square_2$, $\square_3$, $\square_4$, $\square_5$, $\square_6$, $\square_7$, and $\square_8$ in the double log model are different elasticities of the explanatory variables which are measured in different units.

The reason for transforming the equation in double-log model is to pull outlying data from a positively or negatively skewed distribution closer to the bulk of the data in a quest to have the variables be normally distributed.

From the point of interpretation, it is very often to say of which explanatory variable is most important in determining the consumption value from community forest (Y) since the values of estimators like $\square_1$, $\square_2$, $\square_3$, $\square_4$, $\square_5$, $\square_6$, $\square_7$, and $\square_8$ depend on the choice of units to measure the explanatory variables.

Therefore, standard interpretation of estimators in the model is that one per cent change in 'COSEX' results in the respective estimator say ($\square_1$) change in the expected value of Y while all the predictors are held constant. Thus, the elasticity of 'COSEX' reveals the rate of forest dependency as necessity since the estimator, $b_1 < 1$. In this model we find all b's as necessity except 'VIDMKT' and 'CONNECTY'. The necessity of forest dependency arises because of (i) climatic condition and altitude from the sea level and (ii) non-availability of alternative fuel. For example, when there was no change in the average value of COSEX (rupees 46, 650 per annum), the average value of consumption value from community forest was found to be rupees 25,998 per annum. Hence, the forest dependency in the study area was found to be 55.71 per cent. In other words, when average value of 'COSEX' increased by one percent, the average value of Y would increase by 0.19 per cent at 0.01 level (2-tailed) and vice versa. Thus, the study shows that the dependency of community forest has direct bearing on the total household consumption expenditure and it is highly significant at 0.01 level.

In case of the explanatory variables like 'LANDHO', it has a positive relation which is statistically significant at 0.05 level. This happens because of the limitations as stated in page 9, para 2, line 5. The variable 'EDU' is negatively related and significant at 0.01 level. This is due to the fact that higher level of schooling may have better exit options (Ostrom, 2000) due to high opportunity cost and hence, forest extraction activities may be less attractive for those households. Besides, availability of government sector jobs may well divert people from dependency on forests. A similar finding of Gunatilake (1998) observed that education of the family members was negatively related to forest income in the tropical biosphere reserves in Sri Lanka.

Livestock is sometimes regarded as an asset of the rural community. The average value of livestock per household in the study area is rupees 10, 132 and it is positively related but insignificant to the consumption value from commons. This may be due to the fact that the value of livestock is likely to be skewed among the rural households in the study area. In other words, livestock reared in the plains and foothills may be higher than the livestock reared in the hill terrain.

The dummy variable 'VIDMKT' (distance between house and market) was positively related to consumption from community forests and it was statistically significant at 0.01 level. This indicates that the availability of market nearer the village may divert rural communities from forest dependent activities and other gainful activities due to alternative earning opportunities. At the same time, the rural communities living far away from market may have to depend more on community forests in order to sustain their livelihoods. Gunatilake (1998) also showed similar results in the Sinharaya forest of Sri Lanka.

With regard to the road connectivity, it was observed that it is negatively but significantly related with the consumption of community forests. That means the villages having more connectivity have to depend less on community forests and vice versa. Probably with more accessibility, alternative livelihood options become available for the villagers and as a result dependence on community forest reduces.

In common literature, gender was often used to test the effect of gender difference on the level of consumption in CPRs management (Grossman, 1996). Some experimental studies on the gender and cooperative behaviour indicate that women contribute more than men in managing commons due to greater interdependent utility and altruism. However, in the present study one of the aims was to see whether access to and consumption from CPRs was significantly different between male-headed and female-headed households. It was found that the consumption from CPRs was positively related but not significantly affected by gender issue. This may be due to the fact that there were a very few female-headed households in the study area.

In order to understand the relationship between the extent of rural community's dependency on consumption of different forest products and socio-economic variables, three more regression models i.e., regression on consumption of firewood ($\sum_{i=l}^{312} Y_{1i}$), consumption of timber ($\sum_{i=l}^{312} Y_{2i}$) and consumption of bamboo and other minor forest products ($\sum_{i=l}^{312} Y_{3i}$) were estimated. These are represented as:

$$In\sum_{i=1}^{312} Y_{1i} = \beta_0 + \beta_1 InCOSEX_i + \beta_2 InHSIZE_i + \beta_3 InLANDHO_i$$

$$+\beta_4 InGEN_i + \beta_5 InEDU_i + \beta_6 InLIVECOST_i + \beta_6 InVIDMKT$$

$$+\beta_7 InCONNECTY_i + \varepsilon_i \qquad (3)$$

$$In\sum_{i=1}^{312} Y_{2i} = \beta_0 + \beta_1 InCOSEX_i + \beta_2 InHSIZE_i + \beta_3 InLANDHO_i$$

$$+\beta_4 InGEN_i + \beta_5 InEDU_i + \beta_6 InLIVECOST_i + \beta_6 InVIDMKT$$

$$+\beta_7 InCONNECTY_i + \varepsilon_i \text{ and,} \qquad (4)$$

$$In\sum_{i=1}^{312} Y_{3i} = \beta_0 + \beta_1 InCOSEX_i + \beta_2 InHSIZE_i + \beta_3 InLANDHO_i$$

$$+\beta_4 InGEN_i + \beta_5 InEDU_i + \beta_6 InLIVECOST_i + \beta_6 InVIDMKT$$

$$+\beta_7 InCONNECTY_i + \varepsilon_i \qquad (5)$$

To quantify the magnitude of the effect of forest products on the above explanatory variables, the results are represented in estimated equation form as:

$$In\hat{Y}_{1i} = 14.634* + 0.088* InCOSEX_i + 0.098 InHSIZE_i$$
$$(11.203) \quad (4.579) \quad (0.852)$$
$$+ 0.015 InLANDHO_i$$
$$(0.096)$$

$$+0.367 InGEN_i - 0.590* InEDU_i - 0.006 LIVECOST_i$$
$$(0.318) \quad (-\ 4.566) \quad (0.217)$$

$$+14.427* InVIDMKT_i - 0.387* InCONNECTY_i \qquad (6)$$
$$(12.357) \quad (-\ 5.196)$$
$$R^2 = 0.55 \quad \overline{R}^2 = 0.53 \quad F = 45.372 \quad N = 312$$

$$In\hat{Y}_{2i} = -2.868** + 0.088* InCOSEX_i + 0.015 InHSIZE_i$$
$$(-2.100) \quad (4.375) \quad (0.123)$$
$$+ 0.480* InLANDHO_i$$
$$(3.029)$$
$$+ 1.246 InGEN_i - 0.260** InEDU_i + 0.036 InLIVECOST_i$$
$$(1.031) \quad (-1.929) \quad (1.190)$$

$$+0.628 InVIDMKT_i - 0.046 InCONNECTY_i \qquad (7)$$
$$(0.514) \quad (-\ 0.586)$$
$$R^2 = 0.24 \quad \overline{R}^2 = 0.22 \quad F = 12.161 \quad N = 312$$

And,

$$In\hat{Y}_{3i} = -0.119 + 0.014** InCOSEX_i + 0.053 InHSIZE_i$$
$$(-0.307) \quad (2.371) \quad (1.557)$$

$$-0.004 InLANDHO_i$$
$$(-\ 0.096)$$

$$+0.313 InGEN_i + 0.025 InEDU_i + 0.001 InLIVECOST_i$$
$$(0.915) \quad (0.646) \quad (0.052)$$

$$+1.358* InVIDMKT_i - 0.026 InCONNECTY \qquad (8)$$
$$(3.921) \quad (-1.180)$$

$R^2 = 0.15$ $\bar{R}^2 = 0.13$ $F = 6.582$ $N = 312$

Note: 1. The figures in parentheses are t-values
2. The asterisk symbols (* and **) denote significant at 0.01 and 0.05 level.

The estimated equations show that most of the explanatory variables have the expected signs which are statistically significant at different levels. Out of these three regressions, firewood consumption from community forest appears to be the best model since R^2=0.55 and $\bar{R}^2$=0.53. Therefore, firewood contributes significantly to total household consumption expenditure from forests irrespective of poor and non-poor households. In other words, when average value of 'COSEX' increased by say 10 percent, i.e., around rupees 51,320, the average value of firewood consumption increased by 0.19 per cent at 0.01 level, i.e., rupees 20, 360 and vice versa. Though, the average consumption of timber and minor forest products also show a significant dependency at 0.01 and 0.05 levels to consumption value from community forest but and are comparatively lower than the firewood consumption and the effect on timber and minor forest products were negligible.

Finally, an attempt was made to see the forest dependency between poor $\left(\sum_{i=1}^{196} Y_{jiP}\right)$ and non-poor $\left(\sum_{i=1}^{116} Y_{jiN}\right)$ $In\hat{Y}_{jiN} = 17.443^{*} + 0.115^{**} InCOSEX_i + 0.253 InHSIZE_i$ households. It is represented in equation form as:

$$In\hat{Y}_{jiP} = 11.789^{*} + 0.252^{*}\, InCOSEX_i + 0.185 InHSIZE_i$$
$$(6.136) \qquad (5.270) \qquad (1.253)$$
$$-0.211 InLANDHO_i$$
$$(-0.861)$$
$$+1.215 InGEN_i - 0.503^{*}\, InEDU_i - 5.113E$$
$$(0.974) \qquad (-\ 3.476)$$

$$-02InLIVECOST_i + 10.639 * InVIDMKT_i$$
$$(-\ 0.790) \qquad (5.983)$$

$$-0.259 ** InCONNECTY_i \qquad (9)$$
$$(-\ 2.508)$$

$$R^2 = 0.57 \qquad \bar{R}^2 = 0.54 \qquad F = 29.537 \qquad N = 196$$

And,

$$In\hat{Y}_{jiN} = 17.443 * + 0.115 ** InCOSEX_i + 0.253 InHSIZE_i$$
$$(2.868) \qquad (2.361) \qquad (0.712)$$

$$+0.502 InLANDHO_i$$
$$(1.316)$$

$$+5.982 InGEN_i - 1.404 * InEDU_i - 0.082 InLIVECOST_i$$
$$(1.043) \qquad (-2.860) \qquad (-1.059)$$

$$+23.406 * InVIDMKT_i$$
$$(6.696)$$

$$-0.700 * InCONNECTY_i \qquad (10)$$
$$(-2.984)$$

$$R^2 = 0.49 \qquad \bar{R}^2 = 0.45 \qquad F = 12.574 \qquad N = 116$$

Note: 1. The figures in parentheses are t-values.

2. The asterisk symbols (* and **) denote significant at 0.01 and 0.05 level.

The study shows that the poor households are found to be benefiting more from community forest than non-poor households. The estimator of 'COSEX' of the poor households was found to be 0.25 and it was significant at 0.01 level and for the non-poor households it was 0.12 which was significant at 0.05 level. This dependency if we look at different forest products, the poor stakeholders had the estimators of 0.21 (firewood), 0.03 (timber) and 0.02 (minor forest products), and for the non-poor households the estimators were 0.05 (firewood), 0.05 (timber) and 0.02 (minor forest products) respectively. In other words, the poor households higher dependency is on firewood consumption than the non-poor households. In timber consumption, non-poor households had higher dependency than the poor households. And, in minor forest products, both poor and non-poor households had a similar share. Further, if we see at different minor forest products, it was found that the poor households consumed more of bamboo, leafy vegetables, eatable roots and leaves but the non-poor households had higher consumption of the marketable products like honey, medicinal herbs and seeds and wild animals. Therefore, socio-economic heterogeneity in rural community determines the different level of consumption from the community forest. At the same time, heterogeneity in the extraction of forest products between poor and non-poor households was also observed in the study area since these resources were very significant source of rural livelihood to the Arunachalee people who reside in the ecologically fragile and economically poor State.

6

CPRs: Its Distributional Implications and Rural Livelihood Linkages

In the earlier chapter, we tried to explain the relationship between household socio-economic characteristics and consumption from community forests. Hence, in this chapter, an attempt was made to compare the contribution of community forest that accrues to poor and non-poor households as well as rural livelihood linkages. There are many studies which estimated the gross household income (Jodha, 1986; Pasha, 1992 and Kumar, 2000) but the income data suffered from a lot of errors, as respondents normally hesitated in reporting his/her real income and sources of income. The illiteracy of the respondents in the study area was another obstacle in it. Hence, in order to examine the relative importance of community forest in the household economics, the consumption from them in relation to total consumption was analysed.

CONSUMPTION FROM COMMUNITY FOREST

Community forest plays an integral part in rural household economics. The myth, belief and tradition are centred around the forest and its environment and their dependency on it becomes crucial due to many socio-economic factors like predominance of *jhum* cultivation, lack of road connectivity and transport facility, non-availability to market access, traditional belief etc. Under such circumstances, obviously the rural households are compelled to depend on different forest products. On an average, 55.73 per cent of the consumption expenditure of the households in the study area were derived from the community forest irrespective of poor and non-poor households. The relative dependence i.e., percentage of consumption expenditure of households from common property forest resources in different surveyed villages shows the heterogeneity in their consumption pattern. Table 6.1 reveals the annual consumption of forest products in the surveyed villages/ess of Anjaw and Lohit districts.

It was found that the firewood consumption emerged as the most significant contribution to total consumption expenditure of rural households probably because of the traditional dependence on firewood due to climatic conditions as well as the non-availability of alternative fuels. The overall consumption of firewood from community forest appeared as 78.17 per cent of total consumption value from commons, of which the poor derived 86.09 per cent and the non-poor 69.26 per cent respectively. The consumption of firewood was relatively high in Anjaw district than that in Lohit district particularly among the poor and non-poor households. The firewood consumption of poor households in Anjaw was 87.11 per cent of the total consumption value from commons while in Lohit district, it was 85.71 per cent. In case of non-poor in Anjaw district had 70.38 per cent and in Lohit district it was found as 68.79 per cent. The highest dependency of firewood among the poor households was observed in Brailiang village of Anjaw district and the lowest in Danglat village of Lohit district among the surveyed villages. Among the non-poor households, Tillang Kyong village had the highest percentage of firewood consumption to total consumption expenditure of households while Chireng village of Lohit district being the lowest. In general, rural households in Anjaw district had higher dependency of firewood than their counterparts in Lohit district.

Table 6.1: Annual Consumption of Forest Products in the Surveyed Villages

(in per cent)

Name of Village/Distt.	Economic Criteria	Firewood	Timber	Bamboo & Cane	Leafy Veg.	Others
Kasanglat	Poor	84.16	8.75	4.13	2.62	0.34
	Non-poor	72.18	22.77	1.61	0.95	2.49
Kaniliang	Poor	85.1	4.11	6.66	4.13	0
	Non-poor	51.96	43.08	0.8	1.84	0.31
Brailiang	Poor	93.18	3.39	2.38	1.04	0
	Non-poor	75.77	17.4	0.99	1.44	4.4
Anjaw District	Poor	87.11	6.25	3.99	2.46	0.18
	Non-poor	70.38	24.33	1.3	1.23	2.76
Loiliang	Poor	90.8	4.53	2.27	2.41	0
	Non-poor	73.02	22.16	1.44	1.44	1.94
Danglat	Poor	80.93	13.59	4.24	1.23	0
	Non-poor	70.92	23.93	2.83	1.4	0.92
Soolungtoo	Poor	83.18	11.13	3.38	2.31	0
	Non-poor	67.41	29.33	1.94	1.32	0
Chireng	Poor	87.35	4.73	5.07	1.82	1.02
	Non-poor	43.23	50.65	0.3	1.89	3.92
Karhe	Poor	83.43	13.44	2.83	0.3	0
	Non-poor	67.31	28.19	2.48	0.12	1.9
Tillang Kyong	Poor	87.79	6.45	4.64	0.55	0.57
	Non-poor	80.87	7.32	3.83	0.5	4.28
Lohit District	Poor	85.71	9.29	3.37	1.5	0.13
	Non-poor	68.79	26.24	2.28	0.93	1.76

Source: Survey Data, 2005-06.

With regard to the degree of variability in firewood consumption between poor and non-poor, it is found that the coefficient of variation (CV) of overall firewood consumption for the poor and the non-poor was estimated as 34.39 per cent and 43.56 per cent respectively in the study area. In Anjaw district, we found the CV of firewood for poor households as 26.41 per cent and for non-poor households, it was 28.21 per cent. Similarly, it was found in Lohit district that the CV of firewood consumption for poor households as 20.56 per cent and for non-poor households, it was 29.32 per cent. Thus, as far as firewood consumption is concerned, although the variation is low but there is greater variance in non-poor households both in Anjaw and Lohit districts. The relatively high variability in firewood consumption of non-poor is probably due to availability and affordability of alternative fuel, accessibility of market etc. among some of the non-poor households.

Timber consumption (16.57 per cent) emerged as the second highest contributor to consumption from community forest. The poor households derived timber consumption of 8.49 per cent from community forest while the non-poor resulting 25.67 per cent in the study area. Among the poor households, Danglat village of Lohit district had the highest timber consumption while Brailiang village of Anjaw district had the lowest consumption in the surveyed villages. In case of non-poor households, Chireng village had the highest share of timber consumption and Tillang Kyong village of Lohit district was the lowest. The extent of variability in timber consumption from community forest in the study area, it was found that the CV for overall timber consumption of poor and non-poor households was 123.84 per cent and 106.95 per cent respectively. In Anjaw district, the CV for poor households in timber consumption was 83.22 per cent and it was 71.88 per cent for non-poor households. Similarly, in Lohit district, it was found that the CV for poor and non-poor households in timber consumption was as high as 132.86 per cent and 116.76 per cent respectively. Thus, the poor households in both Lohit and Anjaw districts had higher variation in timber consumption than the non-poor households though the level of variation was higher in Lohit district.

Regarding the consumption of minor forest products (5.26 per cent), the overall CV for the poor and non-poor households in Anjaw district was 111.75 per cent and 79.24 per cent respectively while in Lohit district it was 139.31 per cent for poor and 121.09 per cent for non-poor households. Similarly, the consumption of leafy vegetables, eatable roots and leaves, the non-poor households had high variability than the poor households both in Anjaw and Lohit districts. And in the other products like honey, medicinal herbs and seeds and wild animals hunt, the poor households had higher variability than the non-poor households. Thus, in general, the dependency of poor households on commons was relatively higher than the non-poor households on firewood, bamboo, leafy vegetables, eatable roots and leaves while the dependence of non-poor is relatively higher than the poor households on timber and other groups of forest products like honey, medicinal herbs, seeds and wild animals hunt which can be marketed.

The relative dependency i.e., percentage of consumption expenditure of households from common property forest resources in the surveyed villages of Anjaw and Lohit districts, shows another dimension of this study. The results are presented in Table 6.2.

From Table 6.2, we find that there are some variations of dependence on community forest (in terms of consumption expenditures) among various surveyed villages of Lohit and Anjaw districts of Arunachal Pradesh. The dependency on community forest was relatively high in the surveyed villages of Anjaw district than those in Lohit district. This may be due to two factors, namely (i) concentration of high dense forest area in Anjaw district than in Lohit district (where the percentage of forest area is relatively low) and (ii) relatively high altitude of villages of Anjaw district than those of Lohit district. Thus, we find the evidences that dependency was declining where stock of forest resources was relatively less and degraded whereas dependency increased where such stock was relatively high.

Table 6.2: Percentage of Consumption Expenditure of Rural Households from 'CPRF' in the Surveyed Villages

District	Name of Village	Percentage
Anjaw District	Kasanglat	68.1
	Kaniliang	68.8
	Brailiang	62.55
Total		66.04
Lohit District	Loiliang	44.23
	Danglat	54.53
	Soolungtoo	41.15
	Chireng	75.03
	Karhe	68.16
	Tillang Kyong	64.63
Total		52.44

Source: Survey Data, 2005-06.

Table 6.3: Percentage of Consumption Expenditure of Rural Households from 'CPRF' in the Surveyed Villages on the basis of Different Income Categories

District	Income Group	Percentage
Anjaw	Poor	69.02
	Non-poor	64.03
Lohit	Poor	62.40
	Non-poor	44.13
Total	Poor	64.03
	Non-poor	48.62

Source: Survey Data, 2006-07.

Let us now turn our analysis on the forest dependency among different categories on the basis of poor and non-poor households.

Table 6.3 shows that around 64.03 per cent of the total consumption expenditure of relatively poor households were derived from community forests. On the other hand, 48.62 per cent of the total expenditure were derived from community forests for relatively non-poor categories of rural households. Thus, like the previous findings, we find that the forest dependency, no doubt, decreased with the increase in income but the dependence on community forests for the non-poor household was also quite significant. In other words, the poor derived more benefits from the community forest mainly on non-timber forest products but the dependency on community forest for the non-poor households was quite significant in timber as well as other commercial forest products. This may be due to the easier access to intermediate forest products which benefits non-poor households.

Thus, the socio-economic determinants have direct effect on the nature and level of the benefits derived from commons. However, non-poor households used community forest mainly for extraction of timber and other commercial forest products while the poor households used it mainly for collection of firewood, bamboo, and other minor forest products for self consumption (Figure 6.1).

Figure 6.1 shows that there were large variations in the relative contributions to consumption generated by different community-based forest resources. However, it was not uniform across the different economic categories. For example, the consumption of relatively poor households consisted more of firewood (86.06 per cent), followed by timber (8.49 per cent), and minor forest products (5.43 per cent) which mainly comprised of bamboo and leafy vegetables, eatable roots and leaves etc. On the other hand, the consumption of relatively non-poor households comprised more of firewood (69.26 per cent) followed by timber (25.68 per cent), and minor forest products (5.06 per cent). Therefore, the consumption of firewood and timber emerged as significant contributors to relatively non-poor households. In fact, the study shows that as the income of the households increases, the percentage consumption of timber also increase but the

Fig.: 6.1:Consumption of Different Forest Products in Anjaw and Lohit districts

(in per cent)

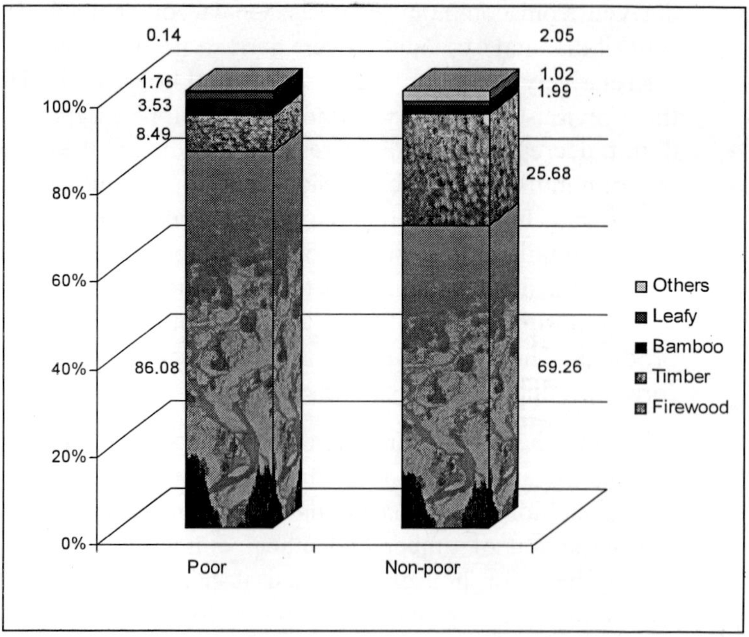

Source: Survey Data, 2005-06.

consumption of other forest products relatively reduces. That means the relatively poor households were depending on community forest for firewood, bamboo and other minor forest products like leaves, medicinal herbs and seeds, vegetables and roots but the relatively non-poor households exploited the community forest more for timber consumption and other forest products which can be marketed.

EMPLOYMENT GENERATION THROUGH ACTIVITIES BASED ON CPRS

The employment generated by CPRs is usually estimated by evaluating the working days spent by a household in the collection of CPR products and in CPR based activities (Singh, 1994 and Jodha, 1986). Eight working hours by an adult person or sixteen working hours by a child have been considered equivalent to one working day (Singh, 1994 and Jodha, 1986). In the surveyed villages of both the districts, women spent more time in CPR based collection of forest products. For example, the percentage of gender-wise days spent in collection of forest products in the surveyed villages was 42.79 per cent for male and 57.21 per cent for female.

Fig. 6.2: Employment Generated through Collecting Forest Products from Community Forest

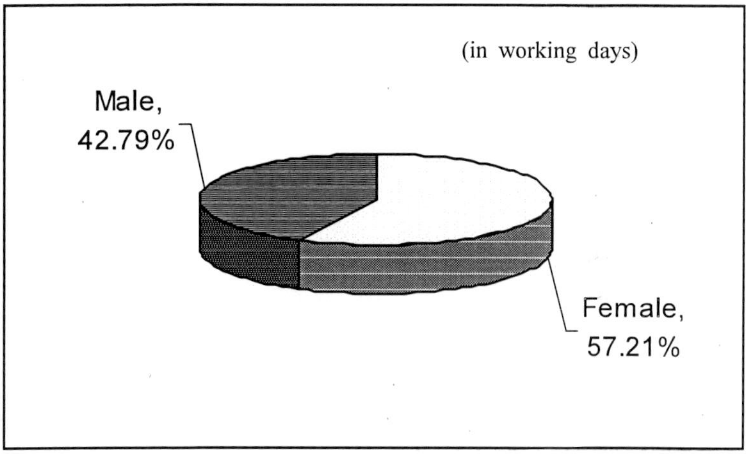

Source: Survey Data, 2005-06.

The females basically spent a number of hours for collection of firewood, leafy vegetables and other minor forest products. The male spent for extraction of timber, hunting of wild animals. The wild animals hunted in the surveyed villages of both the districts comprise mainly of musk deer, wild boar, barking deer, monkey etc. The survey also reveals that womenfolk in the sampled households are engaged not only in management of domestic chores but also in the processing of *jhum* cultivation, storing, utilization and marketing of free bio-mass goods.

CPRs AND RURAL LIVELIHOODS

The question of CPRs and livelihood linkages is essentially on issues of quality of life, diversification of occupation etc. A livelihood, according to Frank Ellis, 'comprises the capabilities, assets (including both material and social resources) gender relations and property rights to support and to sustain a given standard of living' (Ellis, 1998). Multiplicity of livelihood sources help rural households to divert risks and manages uncertainty through allocation of resources. Hence, in this section, an attempt has been made to examine the linkages of CPRs and rural livelihood in the surveyed villages.

Rural households in the study area, make a living and provide their material needs in different ways. They sustained themselves mainly by *jhum* cultivation and were dependent on different forest products from community forest. While some agricultural and forest products like ginger, orange, timber etc. were sold to the market and others were solely for household consumption or bartering with neighbours. All the family members (including husbands, wives and children) contributed their labour to the economic maintenance and survival of the household while the division of labour along gender and age lines were followed in many rural households. The occupational structure outside the household was usually not well-articulated and formalized. Their living were tightly bound up with the household vis-à-vis the community and the economy. The local economy was not something that could be isolated from society. Rather the economy was embedded in the social relations of the family and their community. They undertook a wide range of productive activities. On the farm, they grew crops (the main *jhum* crops in the study area were paddy, maize, millet and *kodo*) reared animals (mainly like mithun, buffalo, cattle, pig, chicken etc.), cleared community forest for *jhum* land, engaged in home-based activities like making basket, mate, repairing or constructing houses and maintained their homestead land. However on the off-firm, they participated in the formal economy through selling or buying of different products in the local market. Their participation in the formal economy comprise only a few facets of economic life in rural areas. They generally participated in informal economic arrangements with neighbours and member of their local communities. One or more may hold full or part-time jobs in the formal economy while other household members may contribute to the economic livelihood of the household by engaging in informal or semi-formal activities, such as selling medicinal seeds (*Subhas Guti*) or handloom products or cardamom or cutting wood.

When informal activities are combined with participation in formal economy in a rural setting a set of interrelated activities obviously generated spanning both the formal and informal sectors of the economy. Some of these sets of activities generate income and some reduce expenses compared to commercial activities. In the rural setting, rural households use the land and CPRs that a household either owns or has access to it. They also use rural skills and accumulated sub-traditional knowledge (for example, how to dribble on the slope of *jhum* land or how to rear animals).

We have identified ten categories of rural livelihood combinations in the different surveyed villages of Anjaw and Lohit districts. These are

(i) Agriculture and Forestry (A+F),

(ii) Agriculture, Forestry and Animal husbandry (A+F+AH)

(iii) Agriculture, Forestry and Business (A+F+B)

(iv) Agriculture, Forestry and Service (A+F+S)

(v) Agriculture, Forestry and Wage labour (A+F+WL)

(vi) Agriculture, Forestry, Animal husbandry and Business (A+F+AH+B)

(vii) Agriculture, Forestry, Animal husbandry and Service (A+F+AH+S)

(viii) Agriculture, Forestry, Animal husbandry and Wage labour

(ix) Agriculture, Forestry, Animal husbandry, Business and Service (A+F+AH+B+S), and

(x) Other combinations.

These attributes, no doubt help to define the character and the range of activities/ occupations in rural livelihood strategies in the surveyed villages of Anjaw and Lohit districts. However, changing abilities of rural household members (as the young member of the family become able to contribute their labour; as adults learn new skills and as adults become old) and changing household composition (through children being born or leaving home for study outside the locality or marriage or divorce or death) make particular activities more or less feasible. Illness or injury of a household member also can have major impacts on their livelihood patterns and thus makes particular livelihood combination inherently unstable. Instability is increased when medical and other health related problems crop up in the family. In such cases, it is reported that they depend on their kith and kin who is in government job or on the local leader. The details are shown in Table 6.4.

The livelihood combinations of Agriculture, Forestry and Animal husbandry (A+F+AH) has the highest frequency (from 6 per cent to 50 per cent). The combination in Kaniliang village was found at 50 per cent, followed by Kasanglat (42.86 per cent) and Brailiang (13.33 per cent) in Anjaw district. In Lohit district, Karhe village had the highest combination (32.14 per cent) followed by Loiliang (28 per cent), Chireng and Tillang Kyong (25 per cent) but Soolungtoo and Danglat villages had 10 per cent and 6 per cent respectively. There were some villages like Kaniliang, Tillang Kyong and Soolungtoo where the combination of four occupations like agriculture, forestry, animal husbandry

Table 6.4: Distribution of Households according to Major Livelihood Strategies in the Surveyed Villages

(in per cent)

Sl. No.	Livelihood Combinations	Kasanglat (Anjaw)	Kaniliang (Anjaw)	Brailiang (Anjaw)	Loiliang (Lohit)	Danglat (Lohit)	Soolungtoo (Lohit)	Chireng (Lohit)	Karhe (Lohit)	Tillang Kyong (Lohit)
1	A + F	3.57	—	—	12.00	5.00	—	16.67	8.93	4.17
2	A+F+H	42.86	50.00	13.33	28.00	10.00	6.00	25.00	32.14	25.00
3	A+F+B	3.57	8.33	60.00	6.67	20.00	14.00	16.67	17.86	16.67
4	A+F+S	7.14	—	—	10.67	7.50	8.00	8.33	3.57	—
5	A+F+WL	—	—	—	8.00	12.50	16.00	—	—	—
6	A+F+H+B	14.29	25.00	—	13.33	15.00	22.00	16.67	16.07	25.00
7	A+F+AH+S	14.29	16.67	20.00	4.00	12.50	14.00	8.33	3.57	—
8	A+F+AH+WL	3.57	—	16.67	2.67	2.50	4.00	—	7.14	8.33
9	A+F+AH+B+S	10.71	—	—	6.67	5.00	8.00	8.33	7.14	8.33
10	Others	—	—	—	8.00	10.00	8.00	—	3.75	12.33

Source: Survey Data, 2005-06.

Note: A= Agriculture, F= Forestry, AH = Animal Husbandry, B = Business, S = Govt. Service, WL= Wage Labour, Others = Other Combinations other than the above combinations.

Table 6.5: Distribution of Households according to Total Number of Livelihood Sources in the Surveyed Villages

(in per cent)

Sl. No.	Livelihood Combinations	Kasanglat (Anjaw)	Kaniliang (Anjaw)	Brailiang (Anjaw)	Loiliang (Lohit)	Danglat (Lohit)	Soolungtoo (Lohit)	Chireng (Lohit)	Karhe (Lohit)	Tillang Kyong (Lohit)
1	Two	3.57	—	13.33	20.00	15.00	8.00	16.67	12.50	16.67
2	Three	53.57	58.33	60.00	53.33	50.00	44.00	50.00	53.57	41.67
3	Four	28.57	41.67	26.67	17.34	27.50	36.00	25.00	19.65	33.33
4	Five	14.29	—	—	9.33	7.50	12.00	8.33	14.28	8.33

Source: Survey Data, 2005-06.

and business are largely found. It is clear from Table 6.3 that a majority of workforce were dependent on agriculture and forestry. However, the percentage of workforce depending upon agriculture and forestry and other different combinations with other occupations varies from village to village. Apart from agriculture and forestry along with the other major occupations there were business and government service also. Thus, we find that the multiplicity of sources of livelihood was a strategy adopted by the households in all the surveyed villages.

On the other hand, the combinations of two or three livelihood strategies reduce expenses associated with particular level of material consumption and the four and the five combinations generate monetary income. Among all the households surveyed, around 49.36 per cent were dependent on three livelihood sources followed by 24.68 per cent in four livelihood, 13.46 per cent in two livelihood sources and 11.54 per cent five livelihood sources respectively. The villages under three livelihood category were Kaniliang (58.33 per cent), Kasanglat (53.57 per cent) and Brailiang (50 per cent) in Anjaw district. In all villages in Lohit district, Karhe village had the highest share having 53.57 per cent, followed by Loiliang (53.33 per cent), Danglat and Chireng (50 per cent), Soolungtoo (44 per cent) and Tillang Kyong (42.67 per cent). In four livelihood sources, Kaniliang had the highest percentage (41.67 per cent) and Karhe had the lowest percentage with 19.65 per cent. Table 6.4 shows the distribution of households according to the total number of livelihood sources in different surveyed villages of Anjaw and Lohit districts.

The study found that villages nearer to the local market have diversified livelihood strategies while the villages which are at a distance from the market have limited livelihood strategies. For example, the surveyed villages in Anjaw district have limited livelihood strategies. But, the surveyed villages in Lohit district, which are more accessible have diversified livelihood strategies which can generate monetary income to supplement their household consumption expenditure. However, it was found that the expansion of non-farm employment opportunities like business and government service do not necessarily result in lower dependency on forest resources.

Thus, we find that the livelihood diversification strategies of rural households are responses to the emerging constraints as well as opportunities on traditional economies which were gradually being integrated into the market-oriented economy.

7

Conclusions and Policy Implication

The study shows that the property rights formations in Lohit and Anjaw districts of Arunachal Pradesh have undergone substantial changes over the last many years. After Independence, there was gradual transformation to monetization. Commercialization and subsequent differentiation led to the emergence of private property in land and forest resources in a limited scale in certain areas. The process continued with the active help of the State machinery. However, with the transformation of the economy from the non-monetised to the monetised on the one hand and the transformation of tribal society on the other, the Common Property Forest Resources (CPRF) in some areas of Lohit and Anjaw districts assumed the nature of 'Open access'. As a result, there was massive destruction of community forest. There were also instances of increasing privatization of community forests. The study found that the 'CPRF' are crucial for the survival as well as the livelihood of the rural households and betterment of environment in the study area. Thus, in order to ensure the sustainable use of 'CPRF', establishment or improving the effective management of CPRs and its equitable distribution have become formidable challenges before us. Hence, the present chapter is an attempt in dealing with such challenges.

Many theoretical frameworks have been formulated and used to understand the management of CPRs. Most popular among them are 'Cost Approach' of Buchanan and Tillocks (1965), Olson's logic of collective action (1965), Game theory approach and recently devised model of Oakerson (1992). Among these frameworks, Oakerson's model has been found most appropriate due to its clarity and adaptability to fit in any situation. Hence, the analytical framework formulated by Oakerson was used here to diagnose and analyse the prevailing CPR management in the surveyed villages of Lohit and Anjaw districts of Arunachal Pradesh.

The slightly simplified and altered form of Oakerson's model isdiagrammatically presented in Figure 7.1.

Fig. 7.1: Oakerson's Model of CPR Management

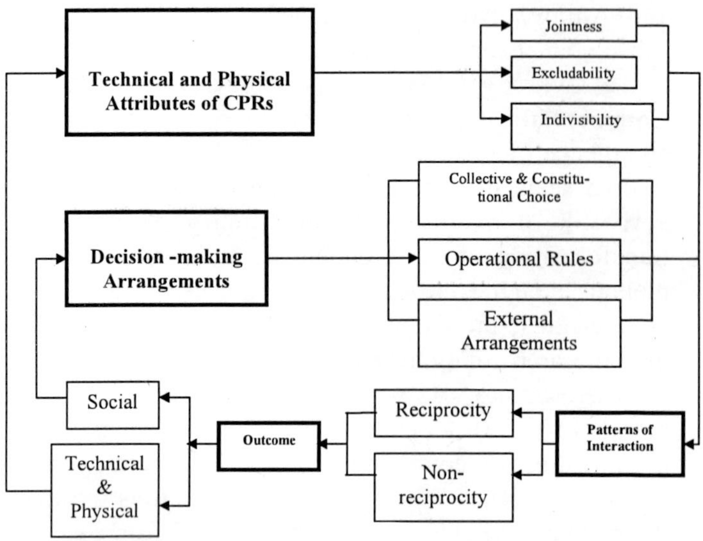

It is evident from Figure 7.1 that the model consists of four components, namely (i) technical and physical attributes of CPRs (ii) decision-making arrangements (iii) patterns of interaction and (iv) outcomes or consequences. In order to examine the technical and physical attributes of CPRs, the model uses three concepts 'jointness', 'excludability', and 'indivisibility'. The decision-making arrangements have been put into three sub-sets:

(i) 'collective and constitutional choice mechanisms',

(ii) 'operational rules', and

(iii) ' External arrangements'.

The pattern of interaction (third component of the model) reflects the behaviour of users and other decision-makers in relation to CPRs and its managements. The success of joint use of CPRs depends on absence or presence of reciprocity amongst the users. The model suggests the use of criteria of 'efficiency' and 'equity' to examine the outcomes. However, the different scholars have emphasized that the outcomes of CPR management should be evaluated in social, economic, physical and situational contexts. Therefore, the criteria of 'sustainability', 'equity', 'equality', and 'user satisfaction' should be used (Adhihari, 2001; Ostrom, 1990; Singh et al, 1996). An attempt has been made to examine the outcomes of existing CPR management in the surveyed villages of Lohit and Anjaw districts of Arunachal Pradesh by using four criteria i.e., sustainability, equity and equality, efficiency. However, the precise measurements of these criteria are quite difficult because of problems in their practical applicability and lack of information.

Chapter five of the present study shows that the dependency on community forests has direct bearing on the total household consumption expenditure and it is highly significant at 0.01 level (2-tailed). The estimator of COSEX (0.19) here indicates the necessity of dependence of rural stakeholders on community forest. Thus, the study reveals that if the consumption value from community forest is increased by one unit from its mean value of 26 units, there is 99 per cent probability of increasing the total expenditure of the household by 1.79 per cent from the mean value 46.65 units and vice versa. Again, among the different forest products, rural stakeholders depend more on firewood (0.09) followed by timber (0.08) and minor forest products (0.02) like bamboo, leafy vegetables, eatable roots, leaves, honey, medicinal herbs and seeds and wild animals etc. The firewood and timber consumption are statistically significant at 0.01 level while the minor forest products is significant at 0.05 level. Thus, firewood consumption emerges as the most significant contribution to total consumption expenditure of the households probably because of the traditional dependence on firewood due to climatic conditions as well as the non-availability of alternative fuel. Moreover, the consumption patterns of different community forest products between the poor and the non-poor households reveal another dimension of the study. The estimator of 'COSEX' of poor (0.252) and non-poor households (0.115) reveal that the responsive changes in consumption value from community forest (Y) with respect to the consumption expenditure for poor households is greater than the non-poor households. Therefore, it is evident that poor households have higher dependency of community forest than the non-poor households. At the same time, when we compare the consumption pattern of different forest products of poor and non-poor households, it was found that the poor households had high firewood consumption than the non-poor households while the non-poor households had high timber consumption than the poor. In case of minor forest products, both poor and non-poor had similar share.

Chapter six supplements the econometric analysis of chapter five and shows the consumption patterns of forest products in percentage term. For example, it was found that the poor households consumed much less value from community forest than the non-poor households. On an average the poor households derived their consumption expenditure of around rupees 22,000 thousand per annum from community forest while the non-poor households derived around rupees 33,000 per annum respectively. Thus, in terms of absolute contribution to the total consumption expenditure of the rural households, community forest contributed more to the non-poor households as compared to the poor households. At the same time, the contribution of the community forest to the household economies was significant in the study area. On an average, 55.73 per cent of the consumption expenditure of the households in the surveyed villages was derived from the community forest. The relatively poor households derived 64.03 per cent of the total consumption expenditure from community forest. On the other hand, 48.62 per cent of the total consumption expenditure was derived from the same source for relatively non-poor households.

Thus, we find that the forest dependency decreased with the increase in total consumption expenditure of the households. It was also found that the poor households had higher consumption on firewood and the non-timber forest products like bamboo, leafy vegetables, eatable roots, leaves than the non-poor households while the non-poor households had high consumption on timber and the non-timber products like honey, medicinal herbs and seeds and wild animals than the poor households. The share of firewood consumption to consumption value from community forest of the poor households was 86.08 per cent and for timber consumption, it was 8.49 per cent. But, minor forest products accounted for 5.43 per cent of the consumption value from community forest of which bamboo had a share of 3.53 per cent, leafy vegetables, eatable roots and leaves had a share of 1.76 per cent, 0.14 per cent respectively. In case of the non-poor households, the share of firewood to consumption value from community forest was 69.26 per cent followed by timber (25.68 per cent), bamboo (1.88 per cent), leafy vegetable (1.02 per cent), and honey, medicinal herbs/seeds and wild animals (2.05 per cent). Thus, the non-poor households exploited the community forest more of timber than the poor households. The study also shows an interesting fact that the extraction of market-oriented products from community forest did not necessarily decrease with the increase in income. Instead we find the evidence that the exploitation of market-oriented products is increasing with the increase in income in the surveyed villages of Lohit and Anjaw districts of Arunachal Pradesh where the stock of natural resources are high. The study shows that the prevailing CPR management in the surveyed villages led to the emergence of 'Neo-rich' class in the study area. This has created not only the inequality among the rural households but also created environmental degradation.

Three types of interaction were observed between users and other decision-makers in the surveyed villages. These are (i) among the users themselves, (ii) between users and village chief or *Gaon Burah* who played an important role in CPR management and collective action, and (iii) between users and various functionaries of the State. The interaction among users with respect to CPRs were characterized by free riding, reciprocity or cooperation which was ingrained among the stakeholders of the study area. However, it was reducing gradually due to monetization of the economy. There was also a growing tendency of privatization of community forest among the non-poor households.

The community or *Village Council* (which is called by the *Taraons* or *Tawarahs* as *Kebeya* or *Pharari* by the *Kamans*) headed by the *Village Chief* or *Gaon Burah* played an important role for decision-making, conflict resolution and collective action on CPR management in the surveyed villages. However, its role was found to be declining particularly in the context of privatization of resources in the surveyed villages.

Thus, the foregoing analysis of prevailing CPR institutions has clearly revealed that the traditional mechanism which maintained balance between man and environment has weakened. In fact, the tribes of the surveyed villages had their own system of forest conservation and management system because they were virtually connected with the preservation of community forest which reflected the age-old pattern of coexistence between man and nature. For example, the majority of the tribes in the study area had strong belief about the presence of supernatural power inside the forest and hence, they often took to perform special rituals associated to it. However, these beliefs are shrinking as the people are coming in contact with modern belief system.

In fact, the traditional property rights formation which was largely collective, are being replaced by private property rights over land and forest. In the traditional phase, apart from the State control over cultivable land and forest, three different types of ownership of land were present in the study area i.e., collective ownership by village communities, clan ownership and private and individual ownership. These ownership rights are not properly recognized by the State but informal ownership through habitual users rights exhibit a great deal of diversity and adaptability. The collective ownership is not just being replaced by private ownership, the meanings and function of the traditional property rights structure have also undergone a significant transformation. In our surveyed villages, we noticed the emergence of private property rights over land and forest and hence it is the most fundamental challenge before us to design a new or dynamic CPR management system so that the forest resources can be used on equity and sustainable basis.

Many collective action theorists have advocated that if a group of individuals are placed in a situation in which they could all mutually benefit by complying the rule of restricted CPRs use, they will not cooperate without external enforcer. Therefore, these scholars have strongly recommended for a change in CPR structure wherever the resources are of the nature of commons.

On the other hand, the scholars associated with 'new institutionalism' have strongly criticized the argument presented by the proponents of change in the property rights of CPRs. They have advocated that user community can use and manage the CPRs in a sustainable way without any external coercion, defying the above mentioned classifications of approaches to solve the CPRs problem. It has been realized that there is no universal solution to the problem as the success or the failure of a management system which depends on a great variety of situation specific factors. An institutional option which best fits in one situation may not be applicable in other settings. Hence, an attempt is made to explore the best fit institution to manage the CPRs in the study area by taking into account the location specific factors.

The forest area of the surveyed villages can be classified into three namely, (i) State Forest (ii) Unclassified State Forest and (iii) Community or Clan Forest. The villagers claimed that the Unclassified State Forest is also Community Forest. In our study area, the Government's initiative to protect and develop CPRs by extending the State Forest Programme like Joint Forest Management was found.

However, it is found that illegal extraction of CPRs (firewood, timber, bamboo etc.) is a common phenomenon in the surveyed villages. Thus, the conversion of CPRs into State property had failed to fulfill its objective to regulate the commons. At the same time, the empirical evidences from the surveyed villages showed that the growing tendency of privatization of CPRs had led to an increasing inequality in the distribution of natural resources.

Hence, as an alternative to both market and State controlled institutional arrangements, local level decentralized management of CPRs should be emphasized. In this connection, it is noted that the indigenous tribes, in the study area, had their own system of forest management where the age-old traditional institution headed by *Gaon Burah* or *Village Chief* played an important role in management of CPRs in terms of resource allocation mechanism, sanction and enforcement rules. However, much of its importance has been lost due to modernization and introduction of monetary economy. Further, the importance of the age-old traditional institution is at stake due to the introduction of village Panchayat system and increasing interference of the State functionaries.

Our theories and experiences based on the case studies show that in many situations, though not always coordination and leadership problems play a dominant role. When the poor households overexploit local resources, they are aware of the ecological impact of their actions. It is often because they face acute survival constraints which lead them to discount streams of future benefits heavily. They generally need externally provided economic incentives to conserve the resources. An external catalytic role by the State via local level institutions can play a significant role. Hence, in the context of Arunachal Pradesh, the sustainable CPR management is only possible through decentralized management with active participation of local stakeholders. The CPRs can never be managed unless the rural households are made to feel that they have a say in their matter.

The study reveals that CPRs play a very important role in the economy of the surveyed villages although the consumption value from community forest is higher for the non-poor households in absolute terms yet in relative terms, the poor households' dependency on community forest is very important and crucial for their survival. Hence, there is urgent need to form sustainable management of CPRs, particularly the forests in order to avoid 'the tragedy of commons'.

Secondly, there is an urgent need to strengthen the age-old traditional system of village council headed by *Gaon Burah* or *Village Chief* in addition to the village Panchayat with specific purpose of management of these resources.

Finally, the success of restoration and sustainable use of CPRs depends on the overall socio-economic development of the rural masses.

Hence, it calls for higher agricultural productivity through modernization of agriculture along with the expansion of horticulture so as to reduce the degree of forest dependency to some extent. It should be noted that any policy intervention to ensure livelihood security of rural communities in Arunachal Pradesh has to be based on a properly framed institutional strategy particularly in relation to the CPR management.

APPENDICES

APPENDIX I

Standard Definitions of the Components of CPRs

1. BUL refers to 'Barren and unculturable land'. It is the area not available for cultivation like land covered by buildings, water, roads, mountains, railways, deserts, otherwise appropriated for non-agricultural purposes.

2. PPGL refers to 'Permanent pasture and other grazing land'. It covers all grazing lands whether they are permanent pastures and meadows or not and village common grazing lands.

3. CWL refers to 'Culturable waste land'. It includes all land available for cultivation but not taken up for cultivation once but not cultivated during the year and the last five years or more in succession.

4. OTCF denotes to 'Other than current fallow'. It includes land lying fallow for more than one year but less than five years.

5. CPRL refers to 'Common Property Land Resources'. It includes BUL, PPGL, CWL and OTCF.

6. CPRF refers to 'Common Property Forest Resources'. It includes 'Protected' and 'Unclassed forest'.

Source: Government of India, 2000: *Wastelands Atlas of India*, 2000, Department of Land Resources, Ministry of Rural Development, New Delhi.

APPENDIX II

Descriptive Statistics of the Explanatory Variables

	Poor		Non-poor		Total	
Variables	Mean	S.D	Mean	S.D	Mean	S.D
Y_{ij}	21.93	7.73	32.88	14.66	26	12.05
COSEX	34.24	10.76	67.62	25.8	46.65	24.08
HSIZE	5.28	2.84	5.71	3.4	5.44	3.07
LANDHO	3.77	1.73	5.85	2.89	4.54	2.45
GEN	0.87	0.34	0.97	0.18	0.9	0.3
EDU	2.42	2.73	2.61	3	2.49	2.58
LIVECOST	2.54	6.41	22.96	13.88	10.13	13.95
VIDMKT	0.25	0.43	0.26	0.44	0.25	0.44
CONNECTY	4.03	6.97	4.28	6.98	4.12	6.96
FIREWOOD	19.13	6.85	22.77	9.92	20.32	8.15
TIMBER	1.61	1.51	8.44	9.03	4.31	6.6
MINOR	1.19	1.67	1.67	1.89	1.37	1.77
N	196		116		312	

Source: Survey Data, 2005-06.

APPENDIX III

Determinants of Consumption from Community Forest

Variables	Coefficient	Standard Error	t-value
Constant	11.646*	1.944	5.992
COSEX	0.190*	0.029	6.624
HSIZE	0.165	0.171	0.969
LANDHO	0.490**	0.225	2.173
GEN	1.927	1.719	1.12
EDU	- 0.825*	0.192	-4.295
LIVECOST	0.043	0.043	0.992
VIDMKT	16.413*	1.737	9.447
CONNECTY	- 0.458*	0.111	-4.139
R^2 = 54	Adj. $\bar{R}^2$ = 53	F = 44.356	N=312

Note: 1. The figures in parentheses are t-values.

2. The asterisk symbol (* and **) denote significant at 0.01 and 0.05 level.

APPENDIX IV

Determinants of Consumption from Community Forest by Forest Products

Variables	Firewood			Timber			Minor		
	□	S.E	t-value	□	S.E	t-value	□	S.E	t-value
Constant	14.634*	1.306	11.203	- 2.868**	1.366	- 2.100	- 0.119	0.387	- 0.307
COSEX	0.088*	0.019	4.579	0.088*	0.020	4.375	0.014**	0.006	2.371
HSIZE	0.098	0.115	0.852	0.015	0.120	0.123	0.053	0.034	1.557
LANDHO	0.015	0.151	0.096	0.480*	0.158	3.029	- 0.004	0.045	- 0.096
GEN	0.367	1.156	0.318	1.246	1.208	1.031	0.313	0.343	0.915
EDU	- 0.590*	0.129	- 4.566	- 0.260**	0.135	- 1.929	0.025	0.038	0.646
LIVECOST	0.006	0.029	0.217	0.036	0.030	1.190	0.001	0.009	0.052
VIDMKT	14.427*	1.164	12.357	0.628	1.221	0.514	1.358*	0.346	3.921
CONNECTY	- 0.387*	0.074	- 5.196	- 0.046	0.078	-0.586	- 0.026	0.022	- 1.180
R^2		55			24			15	
Ajd.R^2		53			22			13	
F-statistics		45.372			12.161			6.582	

Note: 1. The figures in parentheses are t-values
2. The asterisk symbol (* and **) denote significant at 0.01 and 0.05 level.

APPENDIX V

Determinants of Consumption for Poor Households from Community Forest

Variables	Coefficient	Standard Error	t-value
Constant	11.789*	1.921	6.136
COSEX	0.252*	0.048	5.27
HSIZE	0.185	0.148	1.253
LANDHO	-0.211	0.245	-0.861
GEN	1.215	1.248	0.974
EDU	- 0.502*	0.144	-3.476
LIVECOST	-0.051	0.065	-0.79
VIDMKT	10.639*	1.778	5.983
CONNECTY	- 0.259*	0.103	-2.508
R^2 = 56	Adj. R^2 = 54	F = 29.537	N=196

Note: 1. The figures in parentheses are t-values.
2. The asterisk symbol (*) denote significant at 0.01 level.

APPENDIX VI

Determinants of Consumption for Non-poor Households from Community Forest

Variables	Coefficient	Standard Error	t-value
Constant	17.443*	6.082	2.868
COSEX	0.115**	0.049	2.361
HSIZE	0.253	0.356	0.712
LANDHO	0.502	0.382	1.316
GEN	5.982	5.734	1.043
EDU	- 1.404*	0.491	-2.86
LIVECOST	-0.082	0.078	-1.059
VIDMKT	23.406*	3.495	6.696
CONNECTY	- 0.700*	0.235	-2.384
R^2 = 49	Adj. R^2 = 45	F = 12.574	N=116

Note: 1. The figures in parentheses are t-values.
2. The asterisk symbol (* and **) denote significant at 0.01 and 0.05 level.

APPENDIX -VII

The Share of Consumption Value of Different Forest Products from CPRs between Poor and Non-poor Households in the Study Area

(in percentage)

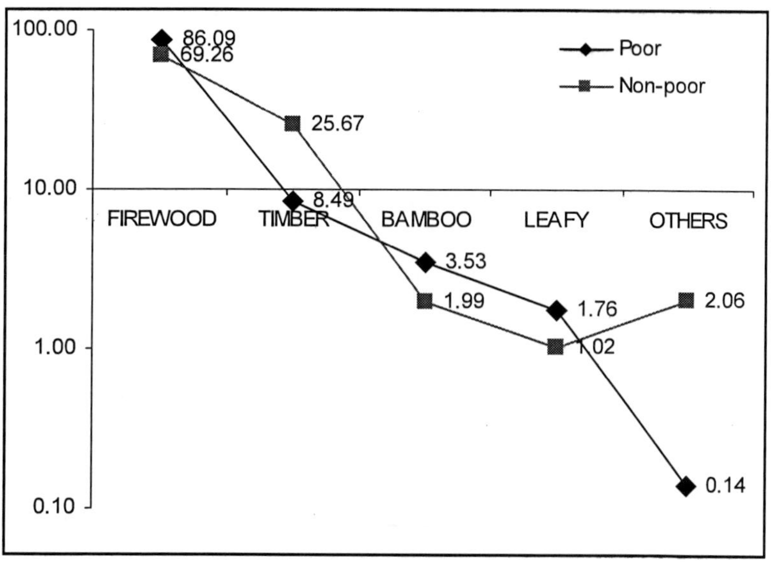

APPENDIX -VIII

The Share of Consumption Value of Different Forest Products from CPRs between Poor and Non-poor Households in Anjaw District

(in percentage)

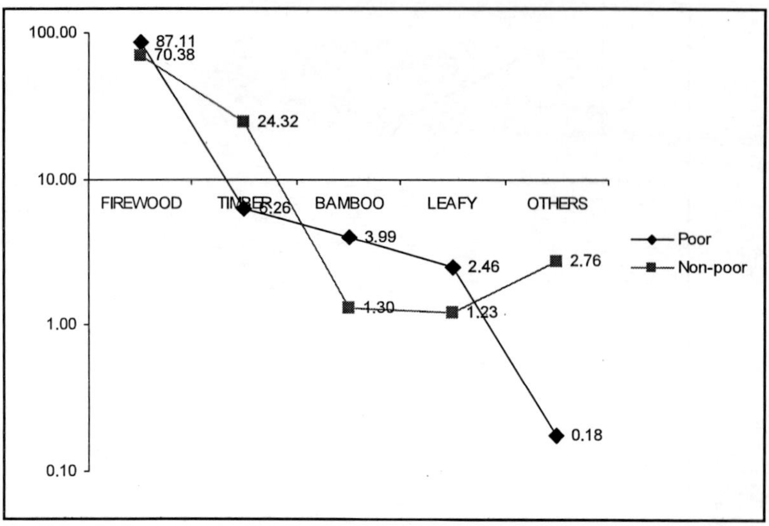

APPENDIX -IX

The Share of Consumption Value of Different Forest Products from CPRs between Poor and Non-poor Households in Lohit District

(in percentage)

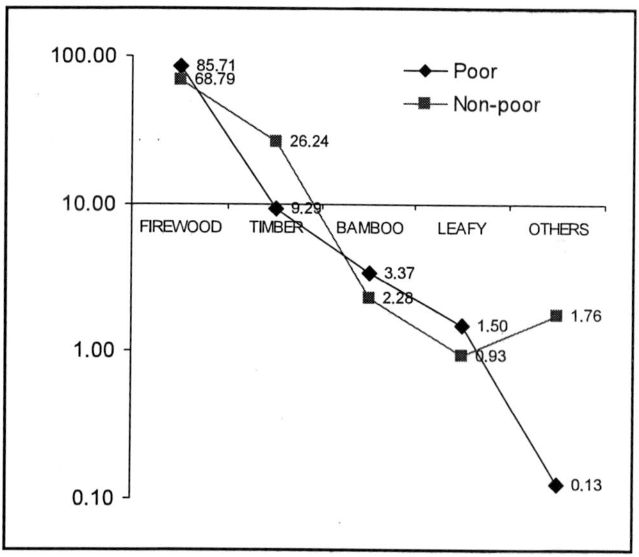

APPENDIX X

Questionnaire for the Household Survey

I. Demographic Information

(i) Name of the District:

(ii) Name of the Block:

(iii) Name of the Village :

(iv) Name of the Head of household:

(v) Name of the Respondent:

(vi) Category (please tick): APST ☐ OTHERS ☐

(vii) Household Characteristics

Sl. No	Name	Age (yrs)	Sex M/F	Relation with HH	Education (no. of schooling year)	Literacy (Yes/ No)	Occupation Code

Code: Agriculture = 1, Govt. Service = 2,Business = 3, Self-employed = 4, Wage labour = 5,Agri + Govt. Service = 6, Agri + Business = 7, Agri + Business +Govt. Service = 8, Agri +Wage labour = 9, Others = 10.

(viii) Are you or your household a migrant to this village?

(Please tick) ☐ Yes ☐ No

If yes, duration of stay in the village? ———— years ——months.

(ix) What are the sources of drinking water?

Source of drinking water	Please tick
Pond	
Spring	
River	
Tap	
Others (please specify)	

(x) Who is the ownership of drinking water sources?

Ownership of drinking water	Please tick
Privately owned	
Community owned	
Government owned	
Others (please specify)	

2. Occupational Patterns and Livelihood Strategy

(i) What are the primary sources of your livelihood?

(Please tick any appropriate livelihood strategy given below)

(a) Agriculture, forestry ☐

(b) Agriculture, Forestry & Livestock ☐

(c) Agriculture, forestry & Service ☐

(d) Others (please specify) ____________________

(ii) Consumer durables in the household

Sl.No	Item (s)	Nos.	Yr. of purchase	Price
i)	Radio			
ii)	TV			
iii)	Audio set			
iv)	VCD/ VCP			

v) Cycle

vi) Gun

vii) Scooter/ Motorcycle

viii) Three/ four wheeler

ix) Furnitures

x) Utencils

xi) Beads

xii) Agricultural tools

xiii) Others (specify)

3. Landholdings, tenure and production system

(i) Land owned/cultivated

Sl.No	Type of land	Total area owned	Land owned privately (area)	Land from village common (area)	Land leased in (area)	Land leased out (area)
i)	Homestead					
ii)	Under jhum					
iii)	Under settled					
iv)	Agri. Land					
v)	Horti. Land					
vi)	Pond					
vii)	Forest					
viii)	Others (specify)					

(ii) Particulars of various crops produced in the past year and annual income from selling agricultural products.

Sl. No	Item	Unit	Unit consumed	Unit sold	Unit price (in Rs)	Total Income (in Rs)
i)	Paddy					
ii)	Wheat					
iii)	Maize					

iv)	Millet
v)	Oil seeds
vi)	Fruits
vii)	Potato
viii)	Ginger
ix)	Turmeric
x)	Pulses
xi)	Vegetables
xii)	Others (specify)

(iii) How long the field crop production can meet your household food demand. (Please tick.)

(a) Less than 3 months

(b) 3 to 6 months ☐

(c) 9 to 12 months ☐

(d) More than a year ☐

4. Collection and Use of Different Forest Products from Community Forests

(i) How much time do you spend in collecting a unit of following forest product?

Sl. No.	Forest products	Unit	Collection time	No. of days/ week	No. of weeks/ month	No. of months/ year
i)	Timber					
ii)	Firewood					
iii)	Bamboo					
iv)	Edible fruits					
v)	Edible roots					
vi)	Seeds					
vii)	Leafy veg.					
viii)	Leafs					
ix)	Medicinal seeds/ plants					
x)	Others (specify)					

(ii) Particulars of Collection and Use of Forest Products from Community Forests:

Sl. No	Forest products	Unit	Produces consumed last year		Amount sold Quantity			Remarks
			Private Forest	Common Forest	Private Forest	Common Forest	Price	
i)	Timber							
ii)	Firewood							
iii)	Bamboo							
iv)	Cane							
v)	Edible fruits							
vi)	Edible roots							
vii)	Seeds							
viii)	Leafy veg.							
ix)	Leafs							
x)	Medicinal plants							
xi)	Others (specify)							

(iii) What are the tools you own that is used in forestry operation and their cost and economic life?

Sl.No.	Type of tools	Cost (in Rs)	Economic life (yrs.)	Percentage of use
i)	Axe			
ii)	Sickle			
iii)	Dao			
iv)	Others (specify)			

(iv) Expenditure incurred in collection of forest products

(a) Expenditure on labour

Types of labour	Labour days used in last one year	Wage paid
Family labour (total)		
Male		
Female		
Paid labour (total)		
Male		
Female		
Others/labour sharing (total)		
Male		
Female		

(b) Other expenditure (if any, please specify)

(v) Animal hunted from the forest during the last one year.

Name of the animal	No.(s)	Amount		Average price in market	Average hours spent for hunting	Distance of hunting area from home	Type of owner ship
		Consumed	sold				

(vi) Livestock owned/ reared

Sl. No	Name	No(s) in the Current yr.	No(s) in the Previous yr.	Current price	Income from selling livestock (if any)
i)	Mithun				
ii)	Cow				
iii)	Bullock				
iv)	Pig				
v)	Goat				
vi)	Sheep				
vii)	Cock & Hen				
viii)	Duck				
ix)	Rabbit				
x)	Others (specify)				

(vii) How do you feed your cattle? Please tick the appropriate answer.

(a) Forest (o)

If yes, who owns the forest? (o)

(b) Grazing land (o)

If yes, who owns the grazing land? (o)

In case of multiple ownership, please indicate the extent of dependence in each of them. (o)

(c) Market (o)

If yes, how much money you spend annually.

(viii) Do you have a livestock rearing shed?

(Please tick) o Yes o No

If yes, what type of shed it is? (Please tick)

(a) RCC o

(b) Semi RCC o

(c) Low cost structure. ○

(d) Thatch ○

(e) Others (specify) ____________________

(ix) What are the benefits of livestock?

Sl.No.	Benefits	Please tick
i)	Source of cash income	
ii)	Milk	
iii)	Meat	
iv)	Wool	
v)	Others (specify)	

(x) Where and how many times do you take your livestock for grazing?

Sl. No	Grazing area	No. of livestock(s)	Season and frequency Summer	Winter	Monsoon	Grazing time
i)	Community forests					
ii)	State forest					
iii)	Grazing land					
iv)	Private land					
v)	Fallow land					
vi)	Others(specify)					

(xi) Please mention the information from the sale of the following livestock products.

Sl. No	Products	Unit	Unit consumed	Unit sold	Unit price (in Rs.)	Total income (in Rs)
i)	Milk					
ii)	Meat					
iii)	Egg					
iv)	Wool					
v)	Others (specify)					

(xii) What are other source(s) of household income other than crop and livestock incomes?

Sl. No.	Source	No. of HH members involved		Annual income (in Rs.)	
		Men	Women	Men	Women
i)	Business				
ii)	Service				
iii)	Cottage industry				
iv)	Wage labour				
v)	Remittance				
vi)	Pension				
vii)	Others (specify)				

(xiii) Do you or any members of the household catch fish? (Please tick.)

o Yes o No

If yes,

(a) From where (name of the water bodies): ....

(b) Who owns the water bodies (specify):.................................

(In case of multiple ownership type indicate the order of importance):................................

(b) No. of days spent for catching fish in last month_______ Year_________

(c) Is there any period when catching fish is prohibited?

If yes, (please specify) ___________________________

(d) The amount of fish sold (if any). ___________________

5. Consumption Expenditure and Household Management System.

(i) Consumption Expenditure of the Household:

Sl. No.	Items	Consumption			Price/ expdt. (if purchased)
		Week	Month	Year	
i.	Rice				
ii.	Wheat				
iii.	Maize				
iv.	Pulses				
v.	Vegetables				
vi.	Chicken				
vii.	Pork				
viii.	Beef				
ix.	Other meat				
x.	Fish				
xi.	Milk (pdr./liq)				
xii.	Country liquor				
xiii.	Foreign liquor				
xiv.	Other foods				
xv.	Clothing				
xvi.	footwear				
xvii.	Gas				
xviii.	Kerosine				
xix.	Firewood				
xx.	Electricity				
xxi.	Medical Expdr.				
xxii.	Educational Expdr.				
xxiii.	House rent				
xxiv.	Leisure/ Entertainment				
xxv.	Telephone				
xxvi.	Others (specify)				

(ii) Have you or household faced any crisis relating to the shortage of food over the last year?

(Please tick) o Yes o No

If yes, how do you manage to meet the consumption needs?

Source	Please tick
Purchase from the market	
Borrow from the neighbours	
Borrow from the relatives	
Borrow from the same clan	
Depend of forest-based food (go for hunting/ collect eatable roots, fruits and vegetables from the forest)	
Others (please specify)	

(iii) Have you given food grains/ eatables to any other household on credit/ as gift when they were facing a shortage of food crisis?

(Please tick) o Yes o No

If yes,

(a) What is the name of the Head of household? ____________________

(b) What is your relationship with the household? ____________________

6. Miscellaneous

(i) Are you or your family members are associated/ participated in any village-level development organization? (Please tick)

o Yes o No

If yes,

Please provide the information.

Sl. No.	Name of organization	Type (code)	Nature of work*	Number of family members involved		Position held	Remarks
				Male	Female		
i							
ii							
iii							
iv							

Code: Local informal = 1, Local formal = 2, Government = 3, NGO = 4, INGO = 5

* Saving and credit = 1, Conservation = 2 , Agriculture/ livestock production = 3, Women's organization = 4, Village cooperative =5, Others = 6 (specify)

(ii) Do you go to market?

(Please tick) ○ Yes ○ No

If yes, please specify the following

(a) What is the distance from the market? ______________

(b) What things do you sell in the market? ______________

(c) How much do you get from selling of the produce in a month/ year?

Sl. No.	Items	Income
i)	Firewood and fodder	
ii)	Timber	
iii)	Leafy vegetables	
iv)	Roots and fruits	
v)	Thatching grass	
vi)	Grasses	
vii)	Roots and fruits	
viii)	Herbal medicines	
ix)	Fish	
x)	Hunted animals	
xi)	Others (please specify)	

Bibliography

Adhikari, B (2001): 'Socio-economic Heterogeneity and Income Distribution: Evidence from Common Property Resource Management', *Journal of Forestry on Livelihoods*, Vol.1, pp.22-24.

Agarwal, A (2001): 'Common Property Institutions and Sustainable Governance of Resources', *World Development*, Vol. 29, No.10, pp.1649-1672.

Agrawal, A and S Narain (1990): *Towards Green Villages*, Centre for Science and Environment, New Delhi.

Arnold, J E M (1995): *Managing Forests as Common Property*, Community Forestry Paper, No.136, FAO, Rome.

Arnold, J E M and J G Campbell (1986): 'Collective Management of Hill Forests in Nepal: The Community Forestry in Nepal: The Community Forestry Development Project', in National Research Council, *Issue Proceedings of the Conference on Common Property Resource Management*, National Academic Press, Washington, D.C, pp. 425-454.

Arnold, J E M and W C Stewart (1989): Report on Common Property Resource Management in India, Submitted to India Agriculture Division, World Bank, Washington, D.C.

Arnold, J E M and W C Stewart (1990): *Common Property Resource Management in India*, Oxford Forestry Institute, London.

Baland, J and J Platteau (1996): Halting Degradation of Natural Resources: Is there a Role for Rural Communities, FAO, Rome.

Ballabh, V and K Singh (1988): 'Managing Forests through People's Institutions: A Case Study of Van Panchayat in Uttar Pradesh Hills', *Indian Journal of Agricultural Economics*, Vol.43, No. 3, pp.296-304.

Bandyopadhyay, S and P Shyamsundar (2004): 'Fuelwood Consumption and Participation in Community Forestry in India', *World Bank Policy Research Working Paper*, No.3331, pp. 1-31.

Bardhan, P (1993): 'Analysis of the Institutions of Formal Cooperation in Rural Development', *World Development*, Vol.21, No.4, pp. 633-639.

Bardhan, P and J Dayton-Johnson (2000): *Heterogeneity and Commons Management*, Department of Economics, University of California, Berkeley.

Basu, N G (1984): 'Community Forestry and the Local Community, in Strategies and Designs for Afforestation, Reforestation and Tree Planting', Issue Proceedings of an International Symposium on the Occasion of 100 Years of Forestry Education and Research in the Netherlands, Wageningen, pp.193-203.

Basu, N G (1987): *Forests and Tribals*, Manisha Granthalaya, Calcutta.

Beck, T (1994): *The Experience of Poverty: Fighting for Respect and Resources in Village India*, IT Publication, London.

Berkes, F (1991): 'Cooperation for Perspective of Human Ecology', in Berkes, F (ed), *Common Property Resources: Ecology and Community-based Sustainable Development*, International Book Distributors, Dehra Dun.

Berkes, F, D Feeny, B McCay and J M Acheson (1989): 'The Benefits of Commons', *Nature*, Vol. 340. No.13. pp. 91-93.

Bhattacharjee, S (1994), *Politics of a Frontier State*, Omsons Publications, New Delhi.

Brokensha, D (1988): *Report on Village-level Management of Common Property Resources in Karnataka*, Submitted to the World Bank, Washington, D.C.

Bromley, D W (1989a): 'Property Relations and Economic Development: The Other Land Reforms', *World Development*, Vol.17, No. 6, pp. 867-877.

Bromley, D W (1989b): 'Entitlements, Missing Markets and Environmental Uncertainty', *Journal of Environmental Economics and Management*, Vol.17, pp.181-194.

Bromley, D W (1991): *Environment and Economy: Property Rights and Public Policy*, Brasil Blackwell, London.

Bromley, D W (1992): 'The Commons, Common Property and Environment Policy', *Environmental and Resource Economics*, Vol.2, No.1, pp.1-17.

Bromley, D W and M M Cernea (1989): ' The Management of Common Property Resources: Some Conceptual and Operational Fallacies', *World Bank Discussion Paper, No. 57*, World Bank, Washington, D.C.

Buchanan, James M and Gordon Tullock (1965): *The Calculus of Consent*, University of Michigan Press, Ann Arbor.

Campbell, J G (1980): *Report on Outstanding Social Issues in the Proposed Madhya Pradesh Social Forestry Project*, Submitted to the U.S. Agency for International Development, New Delhi.

Cavendish, W (1998): *The Complexities of the Commons: Environmental Resources Demands in Rural Zimbabwe*, Centre for Study of African Economics, Oxford University, London.

Cavendish, W (1999): *Poverty, Inequality and Environmental Resource Demands in Rural Zimbabwe*, Imperial College of Sciences, London.

Cavendish, W (2000): 'Empirical Regularities in the Poverty-Environment Relationship of Rural Households: Evidence from Zimbabwe', *World Development*, Vol. 28, No.11, pp. 1979-2003.

Chen, M (1991): *Coping with Seasonality and Drought*, Sage Publications, New Delhi.

Cheung, S N (1970): 'Structure of a Contract and the Theory of a Non-exclusive Resource', *Journal of Law and Economics*, Vol. XIII, pp.49-70.

Chopra, K and S C Gulati (1996): *Environmental Degradation, Property Rights and Population Movements: Hypothesis and Evidence from Rajasthan*, Institute of Economic Growth, New Delhi.

Chopra, K and S C Gulati (2001): *Migration, Common Property Resources and Environmental Degradation,* Sage Publications, New Delhi.

Chopra, K, G K Kadekodi and M N Murty (1989): 'Peoples Participation and Common Property Resources', *Economic and Political Weekly,* Vol. No. pp.189-195.

Choudhury, S D (1978): *Arunachal Pradesh District Gazetteers: Lohit District*, Directorate of Information and Public Relations, Government of Arunachal Pradesh, Shillong.

Chowdhury, J N (1982): *Arunachal Through the Ages: From Frontier Tracks to Union Territory*, Shillong.

Ciriacy-Wandtrup, S V and R C Bishop (1975): 'Common Property as a Concept in Natural Resources Policy', *Natural Resources Journal*, Vol. XV, pp. 713-727.

Coase, R H (1960): 'The Problem of Social Cost', *Journal of Law and Economics*, Vol. III, pp.1-44.

Das, Gurudas (1995): *Arunachal Tribes in Transition*, Vikash Publishing House, New Delhi.

Dasgupta, P (2005): 'Common Property Resources: Economic Analytics', *Economic and Political Weekly*, Vol.XL.No.16, pp.1610-1622.

Dasgupta, P and G M Heal (1979), *Economic Theory and Exhaustible Resources*, Cambridge University Press, Cambridge.

Dasgupta, P and K G Miler (1991): 'The Environment and Emerging Development', Issue Proceedings of The World

Bank Annual Conference on Development Issues 1990, Washington, D.C.

Dayton-Johnson, J (2000): 'Determinants of Collective Action on the Local Commons: A Model with Evidence from Mexico', *Journal of Development Economics*, Vol.62, pp.181-208.

Demestz, H (1967): 'Towards a Theory of Property Rights', *American Economic Review*, Vol. 62, No. 2, pp. 347-359.

Di Falco S and C Perrings (2003): 'Crop Generic Diversity, Productivity and Stability of Agro-Ecosystems: A Theoretical and Empirical Investigation', *Scottish Journal of Political Economy*, Vol. 5, No. 2, May.

Diegues, Antonio C (2000): 'Commons and Protected Areas in Brazil', Presented at the Eighth Conference of the International Association for the Study of Common Property, Bloomington, Indiana, pp.1-16.

Dorfman, R (1988): 'The Political Economy of Environment Protection: A Conversation', *Eastern Economic Journal*, Vol.14, pp.205-209.

Edwards, V M and N A Steins (1998), 'Developing an Analytical Framework for Multiple Use Commons', *Journal of Theoretical Politics*, Vol.10, No.3, pp.347-383.

Ellis, F (1998): Rural Livelihood Diversification: Framework and Categories, National Resource Institute, London.

Feeny, D, F Berkes, B J McCay and J M Acheson (1990): 'The Tragedy of the Commons: Twenty-Two years Later', *Human Ecology*, Vol.18, No.1, pp.1-18.

Fernandes, W and G Menon (1987): *Tribal Women and Forest Economy Deforestation, Exploitation and Change*, Indian Social Institute, New Delhi.

Field, A (2000): *Discovering Statistics Using SPSS for Windows*, Sage Publications, London.

Fox, J M (1983): Managing Public Lands in a Subsistence Economy: The Perspective from a Nepali Village, Unpublished Ph D Dissertation, University of Wisconsin, Madisen.

Ganguly, J B (1997): 'Structural Changes in Jhum-based Economy and Growing Inequalities in North Eastern Tribal Society', in M C Behra and N C Roy, (ed), *Trends in Agrarian Structure in the Hills of North East India*, Commonwealth Publishers, New Delhi.

Ghate, R (2004): *Uncommons in the Commons: Community Initiated Forest Resource Management*, Concept Publishing Company, New Delhi.

Gordon, H S (1954): 'The Economics of a Common Property Resource: The Fishery', *Journal of Political Economy*, Vol.62, No.2, pp.124-142.

Government of India (2001): *State Forest Report*, Forest Survey of India, Ministry of Environment and Forest, New Delhi.

Government of India (2001): *Statistical Abstract, India*, Directorate of Economics and Statistics, Ministry of Agriculture and Cooperation, New Delhi.

Government of India (2002): Land use Statistics of India, Retrieved on August 17, 2006 from htpp://www.indiastat.com

Government of India (2004): *Agricultural Statistics at a Glance*, Directorate of Economics and Statistics, Ministry of Agriculture, New Delhi.

Government of India (2004): *Forest and Wildlife Statistics*, Forest Survey of India, Ministry of Environment and Forest, New Delhi.

Government of Arunachal Pradesh (1987): *Statistical Abstract*, Directorate of Economics and Statistics, Shillong.

Government of Arunachal Pradesh (1987): *Statistical Hand-Book of Lohit District*, Economics and Statistics Department, Tezu.

Government of Arunachal Pradesh (1992): *Statistical Hand-Book of Lohit District*, Economics and Statistics Department, Tezu.

Government of Arunachal Pradesh (1994): *District Census Handbook, Lohit*, Census of India, 1991, Series 3, Arunachal Pradesh, Directorate of Census Operations, Itanagar.

Government of Arunachal Pradesh (1995): *Statistical Abstract of Arunachal Pradesh*, Directorate of Economics and Statistics Department, Itanagar.

Government of Arunachal Pradesh (1998): *State Domestic Product of Arunachal Pradesh*, State Income Unit, Directorate of Economics and Statistics Department, Itanagar.

Government of Arunachal Pradesh (2000): *Statistical Abstract of Arunachal Pradesh*, Directorate of Economics and Statistics Department, Itanagar.

Government of Arunachal Pradesh (2001): *Statistical Abstract of Arunachal Pradesh*, Directorate of Economics and Statistics Department, Itanagar.

Government of Arunachal Pradesh (2002): *Statistical Abstract of Arunachal Pradesh*, Directorate of Economics and Statistics Department, Itanagar.

Government of Arunachal Pradesh (2002): *Statistical Hand-Book of Lohit District*, Economics and Statistics Department, Tezu.

Government of Arunachal Pradesh (2003 & 2004): *Statistical Hand-Book of Lohit and Anjaw District*, District Statistical Office, Tezu.

Government of Arunachal Pradesh (2005): *Arunachal Pradesh, Human Development Report*, Development of Planning, Itanagar.

Government of Arunachal Pradesh (2005): *Statistical Hand-Book of Lohit District*, Economics and Statistics Department, Tezu.

Government of Arunachal Pradesh (2007): Draft Tenth Five-year Plan, Department of Planning, Itanagar, Retrieved on 2nd Jan, 2007 from http://www.arunachalpradesh.nic.in.

Gray, Kevin (1993): 'The Ambivalence of Property', in Gwyn Prins (ed), *Threats Without Enemies*, Earthscan Publications, London.

Greene, W H (2000): Econometric Analysis, Prentice Hall, New Jersey.

Grossman, L (1996): ' The Cultural Ecology of Economic Development', *Annals of Association of American Geography*, Vol.71, pp.220-231.

Guha, R (1989): The Unquiet Woods: Ecological Change and Peasant Resistance in the Himalaya, Oxford University Press, New Delhi.

Gunatilake, H M (1998): 'The Role of Rural Development in Protecting Tropical Rainforests: Evidence From Sri Lanka', *Journal of Environmental Management*, Vol.53, pp. 273-279.

Gunatilake, H M et al (1993): 'Role of Non-timber Forest Products in the Economy of Peripheral Villages of Knuckles National Wilderners Area of Sri Lanka: A Farming Systems Approach', *Economic Botany*, Vol. 47, pp. 275-281.

Hanna, S and M Munasinghe (1995): 'An Introduction to Property Rights and the Environment', in S Hanna and M Munasinghe (ed), *Property Rights and the Environment: Social and Ecological Issues*, World Bank, Washington, D.C.

Hanna, S, C Folke and K Maler (1996): 'Property Rights and the Natural Environment', in Hanna S, C Folke and K Maler (ed), Rights to Nature, Island Press, Washington, D.C.

Hardin, G (1968): 'The Tragedy of Commons', *Science*,Vol.162, pp.1243-1248.

Iyengar, S (1989): 'Common Property Land Resources in Gujarat: Some Findings about Their Size, Status and Use', *Economic and Political Weekly*, Vol. XXIV, No.25, pp. A67-A77.

Jodha, N S (1986a): *The Decline of Common Property Resources in Rajasthan, India*, Overseas Development Institute, London.

Jodha, N S (1986b): 'Common Property Resources and Rural Poor in Dry Regions of India', *Economic and Political Weekly*, Vol. XXI, No.27, pp. 1169-1182.

Jodha, N S (1990): 'Rural Common Property Resources: Contribution and Crisis', *Economic and Political Weekly*, Vol. XXV, No.26, pp. A65- A78.

Kadekodi, G K (2001): 'Environment and Development', in Rabindra N Bhattacharya (ed), *Environmental Economics: An Indian Perspective*, Oxford University Press, New Delhi.

Kadekodi, G K (2004): *Common Property Resource Management*, Oxford University Press, New Delhi.

Koutsoyiannis, A (2001): *Theory of Econometrics: An Introductory Exposition of Econometric Methods*, Second Edition, Palgrave, New York.

Kumar, Sanjay (2002): 'Does Participation in Common Pool Resource Management Help the Poor? A Social Cost-benefit Analysis of Joint Forest Management in Jharkhand, India', *World Development*, Vol.30. No.5, pp.763-782.

Kumar, Suresh (2000): *Common Property, Community Interests and Environmental Concerns*, Manak Publications, New Delhi.

Larson, B A and D W Bromley (1990): 'Property Rights, Externalities and Resource Degradation, *Journal of Development Economics*, Vol.33, No.2, pp.235-262.

Leach, M, R Meams and I Sioones (1999): 'Environmental Entitlements: Dynamics and Institutions in Community Based Natural Resource Management', *World Development*, Vol.27, No.2, pp. 225-247.

Libecap, G D (1989): 'Distributional Issues in Contracting for Property Rights', *Journal of Institutional and Theoretical Economics*,Vol.145, pp.6-24.

McCarthy, N , E Sodoulet and A de Janvry (2001): 'Common Pool Resource Appropriation under Costly Cooperation', *Journal of Environmental and Economic Management*, Vol. 42. No.3, pp. 297-309.

McCay, B (1996): 'Common and Private Concerns' in S Hanna, C Folke, Maler and Karl-Goran (ed), *Rights to Nature: Ecological, Economic, Cultural and Political Principles of Institutions for the Environment*, Island Press, Washington, D.C.

McCay, B and J A Acheson (ed) (1987): *Capturing the Commons*, University of Arizona Press, Tucson.

McCay, B and J A Acheson (ed) (1988): *The Question of the Commons: The Culture and Ecology of Communal Resources*, University of Arizona Press, Tucson.

McKean, M A (1986): 'Management of Traditional Common Lands in Japan', Issue Proceedings of the Conference on Common Property Resource Management, National Academy Press, Washington, D.C.

McKean, M and E Ostrom (1995): 'Common Property Regimes in the Forest: Just a Relic from the Past', *Unasylva*, Vol.46, pp. 3-15.

Menon, A (1999): 'Common Property Studies and the Limits to Equity: Some Conceptual Concerns and Possibilities', *Review of Development and Change*, Vol.4, No.1, pp.51-70.

Mishra, S N (1983): 'Arunachal's Tribal Economic Formations and Their Dissolution', *Economic and Political Weekly*, Vol. XVIII, No.43. pp. 1837-1846.

Mitra, A (1998): 'Environment and Sustainable Development in Hilly Regions of North East India - A Study of Arunachal Pradesh', *International Journal of Social Economics*, Vol.25, No.24, pp. 196-206.

Mitra, A (1999): 'Planning for Forestry and Environment Development in Arunachal Pradesh', in A Banerjee and B Kar (ed), *Economic Planning and Development of North-Eastern States*, Kanishka Publishers, New Delhi.

Mitra, A (2000): Report on Environment Conservation and Demand for Nature-based Tourism in Arunachal Pradesh, Retrieved on July 05, 2006 from htpp://coe.mse.ac/ eercrep/ abs/ amitava_abs.pdf

Mitra, A (2003): 'Forestry Planning in Arunachal Pradesh - Need for an Alternative Approach', *Assam Economic Journal*, Vol. XV, pp.74-81.

Mitra, A (2006): 'Transformation of Arunachal's Economy: Opportunities and Challenges for a Less Developed State', *Indian Development Review*, Vol.4, No.2, pp.433

Mitra, A and K Chattopadhyay (2003): *Environment and Nature-Based Tourism: An Endeavour at Sustainability*, Kanishka Publishers, New Delhi.

Mitra, A and D K Mishra (2005): *Report on Environment, Property Rights and Rural Livelihood Strategies: A Study on Arunachal Pradesh*, Indian Council for Social Science Research, New Delhi.

Nadkarni, M V et al (1998): *The Political Economy of Forest Use and Management*, Sage Publications, New Delhi.

Nandwani, S C (1975): *Methodology of Economic Analysis*, Cosmopolitan Publishing House, New Delhi.

NCAER (1967): *Techno-Economic Survey of NEFA*, New Delhi.

NEC (1982-83): *Annual Plan*, Shillong.

NEC (2002): *Basic Statistics of North Eastern Region*, Shillong.

North, Douglass C (1990): *Institutions, Institutional Change and Economic Performance*, Cambridge University Press, Cambridge.

NSSO (1999): *Data Documentation for NSS 54th Round*, Department of Statistics, Government of India, New Delhi.

Oakerson, R J (1992): 'Analyzing the Commons: A Framework', in D.W. Bromley (ed), *Making the Commons Work: Theory, Practice and Policy*, Institute for Contemporary Studies Press, San Francisco, pp. 41-59.

Olson, M (1965): *The Logic of Collective Action: Public Goods and The Theory of Groups*, Harvard University Press, Cambridge.

Ostrom, E (1986): 'An Agenda for the Study of Institutions', *Public Choice*, Vol. 48, pp. 3-25.

Ostrom, E (1990): *Governing the Commons: The Evolutions of Institutions for Collective Action*, Cambridge University Press, Cambridge.

Ostrom, E (2000): 'Reformulating the Commons', *Swiss Political Science Review*, Vol. 6, No,1, pp. 29-52.

Otsuka, K and F Place, (2001): 'Toward New Paradigm of Land and Tree Resource Management', in K Otsuka and F Place (ed), *Land Tenure and Natural Resource Management: A Comparative Study of Agrarian Communities in Asia and Africa*, Johns Hopkins University Press, Baltimore.

Pasha, S A (1992): 'CPRs and Rural Poor: A Micro Level Analysis', *Economic and Political Weekly*, Vol. XXVIII, No. 46, pp. 2499-2503.

Pathak, A (1994): *Contested Domains: The State, Peasants, and Forests in Contemporary India*, Sage Publications, New Delhi.

Paul, S (1989): 'Poverty Alleviation and Participation: The Case of Government Grassroots Agency Collaboration', *Economic and Political Weekly*, Vol. XXIV, No. 2, pp.100-106.

Pearce, D (1998): *Economics and Environment: Essays on Ecological Economics and Sustainable Development*, Edward Elgar, London.

Pinkerton, E and M Weinstein (1995): *Fisheries that Work: Sustainability through Community Based Management*, David Suzuki Foundation, Vancouver.

Pinkerton, E *et al.* (1989): *Cooperative Management of Local Fisheries: New Directives for Improved Management and Community Development*, University of British Columbia Press, Vancouver.

Posner, R A (1977): *Economic Analysis of Law*, Mass: Little, Brown & Co., Boston.

Prakash, A and A Gupta (1997): 'Ecologically Sustainable Institutions', in P Smith (ed), *Environmental Sustainability Practical Global Implication*, St. Luice Press, Boca Raton, Florida, pp.47-65.

Priyanka, P (2004): A Study of Property Rights and Production Efficiency in Arunachal Pradesh, Unpublished Ph.D. Dissertation, Rajiv Gandhi University, Itanagar.

Reddy, V R (1999): 'Valuation of Renewable Natural Resources User Perspective', *Economic and Political Weekly*, Vol. XXXIV, No. 23. pp.1435-1444.

Richards, M, K Kanel, M Maharjan and J Davies (1999): *Towards Participatory Economic Analysis by Forest User Groups in Nepal*, Overseas Development Institute, London.

Roy, N C and P K Kuri (1997): 'Changing Property Rights in Land and Agrarian Reforms in Arunachal Pradesh', *Political Economy Journal of India*, Vol.6, pp.71-74.

Runge, C F (1981): 'Common Property Externalities: Isolation, Assurance and Resource Depletion in a Traditional Growing Context', *American Journal of Agricultural Economics*, Vol.63, pp.595-606.

Runge, C F (1986): 'Common Property and Collective Action in Economic Development', *World Development*, Vol.14, No.5, pp.623-635.

Sethi, R and E Somanathan (1996): 'The Evolution of Social Norms in Common Property Resource Use', *American Economic Review*, Vol.86, No.4, pp.766-788.

Shiv, Vandana (1986): 'Coming Tragedy of the Commons', *Economic and Political Weekly*, Vol. XXI, No.15, pp.613-614.

Shiv, Vandana (1991): *Ecology and the Politics of Survival*, Sage Publications, New Delhi.

Singh, A I and S Bhattacharjee (2007): 'Degradation of Common Property Resources in a Market Economy' in N Ali (ed), *Natural Resources and Tribal Communities in North East*, Mittal Publications, New Delhi.

Singh, Chatrapati (1986): *Common Property and Common Poverty: India's Forests, Forest Dwellers and the Law*, Oxford University Press, London.

Singh, K, N Singh and R P Singh (1996): 'Utilisation and Development of Common Property Resources – A Field Study in Punjab', *Indian Journal of Agricultural Economics*, Vol. 51, No.1&2, pp.249-259.

Singh, Kartar (1994): *Managing Common Pool Resources: Principles and Case Studies*, Oxford University Press, New Delhi.

Somanathan, et al (2002): *Collective Action for Forest Conservation: Does Heterogeneity Matter*? Indian Statistical Institute, New Delhi.

Steins, N A, and V M Edwards (1999), 'Collective Action in Common Pool Management: The Contribution of a Social Constructivist Perspective to Equity Theory', *Social and Natural Resources*, Vol.12, pp.539-552.

Steins, N A, V M Edwards and Niels Rolling (2000), 'Redesigned Principles for CPR Theory', *The Common Property Resource Digest*, No.53, pp.1-4.

Tang, S Y (1991): 'Institutional Arrangements and the Management of Common-Pool Resources', *Public Administration Review*, Vol.51, No.1, pp.42-51.

UNDP (2001): *Human Development Report*, New York.

Uphoff, N (1986): Local Institutional Development: An Analytical Sourcebook with Cases, Kumarian Press, West Hartford.

Uphoff, N (1993): 'Grassroots Organisation and NGOs in Rural Development: Opportunities with Diminishing States and

Expanding Markets', *World Development*, Vol.21. No.4. pp. 607-622.

Wade, R (1987): 'The Management of Common Property Resources: Collective Action as an Alternative to Privatisation or State Regulation', *Cambridge Journal of Economics*, Vol.11, pp. 95-106.

Weitzman, M (1974): 'Free Access vs. Private Ownership as Alternative Systems for Managing Common Property', *Journal of Economic Theory*, Vol. 8, No. 2, pp.225-234.

Wells, M and K Bradon (1992): *People and Park: Linking Protected Area Management with Local Communities*, World Bank, Washington, D.C.

World Bank (1992): *World Development Report: Development and the Environment*, Oxford University Press, New York.

Yanggen, D and T Reardon (2001): 'Kudzu-improved fallows in the Peruvian Amazon', in A Angelsen and D Kaimowilze (ed), *Agricultural Technologies and Tropical Deforestation*, CABI Publication in Association with Centre for International Forestry Research, Bogor, pp.213-229.

Introduction